BOREDOM BUSTERS

Turn everyday moments into creative memories.

BY BARBARA VOGELGESANG
ILLUSTRATED BY EMMA ENGLER
Hawkvale Publishing 2020

To my husband Jim

and to my children

Nicholas, Libby, Sarah, and Alex,

for providing me with the honor

of being called Mom.

Contents

PERSONALLY SPEAKING

Prior to my life as a mom, I had the thrill of traveling with Ringling Bros. and Barnum & Bailey Circus. Yes, you read that correctly. I was a clown in the Greatest Show on Earth. While I was there, I met families from all over the world and observed their parenting from a ringside seat. Circus families are, in some ways, just like our families, but they have a different focus. They don't worry about laundry, grocery shopping, housekeeping, and cooking. Those chores need to be done, but circus mamas don't think about them day in and day out. Chores are not the focus of their days. They are passing on family traditions, celebrating moments, and using every experience to educate and bind their families together.

Early in life circus families teach their children their profession. I remember a juggler we worked with who practiced constantly. We would often see his preschooler throwing a ball up and down, "practicing" beside his Dad. Now, 20 years later, that young man is performing around the world at the most prestigious theaters as his father's partner. They are an awesome team who perform well together and have become not only a great father/son team but close friends.

Circus children are encouraged to stretch their limitations. They are praised for working hard and accomplishing a new skill. The only time I remember a parent discouraging a child from trying something difficult was when doing so would put them in danger. During my first year with Ringling Bros., all the adults were treated to a private circus starring the circus children. The entire cast showed up and enthusiastically applauded for each child's act. After the show, various performers helped mentor the children in their interests. There are no age divisions on the road. Children of all ages work and play together with adults they respect and seek to emulate. There is nothing like seeing children from many different cultures, in various costumes, doing schoolwork backstage.

We celebrated everything on the circus. Birthdays, holidays, different cultural festivities, accomplishments, and even animal birthdays were a reason to party. It gave the children of all ages something to look forward to. Believe it or not, life on the road can get just as monotonous as being in one place, especially if that is all you have ever known. Circus Mamas have a lot in common with town moms. Most kids with working moms watch her put on her makeup every morning, as a clown my makeup was just a little more extensive and involved a red nose.

Traveling meant exposure to many wonderful sights. Circus families do their best to take advantage of this. We all knew we may never get to this town or country again. On our time off many of the families completed chores and practice as quickly as possible to be able to tour around. Walking around the battlefield in Gettysburg makes it a lot easier to remember what happened there.

Shortly after I conceived my second child, my husband Jim, and I decided to run away from the circus to establish a home. Suddenly I found my mothering swallowed up by housekeeping, the laundry, cooking, garden chores, and endless running around. That wasn't why I wanted to be a mother. When I got together with other mothers, they spent more time discussing presoaking stains than playing with their children. It sounded to me like many parents looked at their children as another chore on the list. This broke my heart and I didn't want to fall into that philosophy.

I took the matter to God in my prayer time. He reminded me of those circus families. My focus needed to shift. Could it? On the circus, our "homes" were so small -- trailers, motor homes, and twenty by six-foot living compartments on a train. We didn't have as many clothes because we spent so much time in costume. On and on the doubts surfaced, but I was determined in spite of them. I was not going to let my chores cheat my children and me out of the fun of mothering. We are all just one small adjustment from making our lives work. Celebrating my children and enjoying life as a mother was worth the adjustments that needed to be made. Adjustments in my mindset, my attitude, and my point of view would benefit my family in ways I hadn't even thought possible.

I shared my thoughts and ideas with other moms. Many of them caught my excitement. Creativity begot creativity. Soon, instead of new window cleaners, we were discussing new games we had tried. We discovered fun ways to include our children in the activities around our homes. We sought out local sights and happenings that we could expose our little ones to. The best part of all was that we could do all of this inexpensively. Our children were happier. We were happier. Even our husbands were happier.

As my children grew, I noticed they had absorbed this joyful way of living. If something was hard to learn, they looked at it as a challenge to overcome instead of being discouraged. I watched them turn to each other as well as my husband and me for support and inspiration. They grew to be confident people who know the home team is always going to show up to cheer for them...even if they fail. When they do fail each of my kids knows they have the rest of us to help pick them up.

Housekeeping, for most of us, is boring. Our children get bored watching us do it. They get weary of hearing us nag them to help. Children get tired of the same toys, the same videos, the same everything day in and day out. Sometimes they get bored for no reason.

It's been 27 years and four children since I first become a mom. I am often complimented on my "successful family." We are a close-knit family who likes to laugh, learn, encourage, and play together. My adult kids stay in close contact with their younger siblings whether they are college or at home. Life has changed so much over the years. I'm not performing much anymore but I am still working and there are days when I desperately need to know there is fun, magic, and joy waiting for me at home. We don't have to look at our lives as a stretch of days one just like another. Let's bust the boredom and celebrate these family moments. Parenting is an exciting adventure: one in which we are challenged to create marvelous memories, celebrate memorable moments, and have fun with our families. Family can and should be our happy thoughts that enable us to fly. We can do it!

Joyfully,

Barbara

Acknowledgments

This little book would not be a reality without the support and encouragement of so many dear people.

To my husband, Jim, thank you for your love and for letting me have my crazy schemes. I am so blessed to have such a great partner in crime who lets me stay home with our children and write and provides for our family.

To Nicholas and Libby, it was great fun trying out all of these crazy ideas for the first edition of Boredom Busters. You went along with the ones that worked and helped me laugh through the ones that didn't. Thanks for being such willing guinea pigs when you were little and amazing cheerleaders now that you are grown.

To Sarah and Alex, thanks for being the amazing kids that you are. You are patient with me when I'm trying to write and in my own little world. You help me to remember to play. I couldn't ask for better playmates who grew up to be treasured friends.

Thank you to the talented Emma Engler for creating this fun cover for Boredom Busters and to Kristin Engler for being such a wonderful encourager.

To all the incredible friends I have made through MOPS International. Many years have passed since the first publication of this book and you are still giving me vision and encouragement. Thank you.

To all the moms and dads, I've met on this exciting adventure called life. You are my fellow travelers on this parenting journey. Together we can give our children a wonderful childhood and support each other in this sometimes-troubled world.

Beat Boredom with an Attitude of Celebration

Children are spontaneous creatures and live in the now. They are really good at open-hearted, spontaneous joy. They don't put it on hold. Anyone who has been lucky enough to receive a muddy hug or a sticky kiss knows that. Children spend joy with abandon. They know the more joy you spread, the more you will have. Children are pros at the art of celebration. They practice it on every small occasion. An adult who grows up celebrating life will find their days are much more fulfilling. Why shouldn't parents join the party?

Shift your focus.

We have all heard that a child's work is play. Unfortunately, we often forget our children's need to play -- and our own need to play -- by rushing past it. We move too fast and miss the joy of life as it was intended to be experienced. Sometimes we need to shift our focus, to look past the surface and see the whole of life, not just today. It's so hard to not let the to-do list or outside appointments keep us from snuggling, tickling, and telling bad knock-knock jokes. The reality is that years from now we'll remember the knock-knock jokes and forget what was on those lists.

That shift in focus is so crucial when we become parents. My friend Ann and her husband adopted two and four-year-old brothers. She was telling me how neat it is to see Eric relax because of these little guys. They have hardwood floors in their house and Eric treated them like fine furniture. Now that he has these sons, he's on the floor pushing Tonka trucks on those once precious floors. Being connected to his sons is much more important than any floor.

***Make ordinary occurrences extraordinary.**

I look at life as an exciting adventure. Boredom can rob a person of joy. My children get bored and I get bored and life in our house isn't so pleasant. That's when I look for ways to make ordinary occurrences extraordinary.

When my son Nick was five, he had a problem finding things. I sent him to his room to get something and he always came back saying he couldn't find it. There were too many other things to think about and look at on the way from the kitchen to his room. To be honest this drove me crazy. I explained to Nick what a detective did and how they solved mysteries and found lost items. We discussed looking for clues and following up on them. I bought an old fedora hat at a yard sale, made a sign that said, "We leave no stone unturned" and encouraged him to open his own Private Investigation Agency. When I needed him to locate something, I asked him to help me solve a mystery and formed my request like a missing person's report. He loved it and was able to be more helpful to me. Other times I've been known to send out a knight in shining armor to accomplish a quest. Sometimes it's been a "your mission, should you choose to accept it." Suddenly, chores were much more fun for all of us.

***Encourage your children to see the world in a unique way.**

Try to find ways to encourage your children to see the world in a more interesting, exciting, and fun light. Laughter is a gift of God that brightens our good times and lightens the rough ones. Enjoy your children. Most kids are really funny.

Probably because my children were raised by two clowns, they have an incredible sense of humor and tend to look for creative solutions to problems.

Children's imaginative worlds become testing grounds where they perfect their socialization skills, try out future careers, and learn to think outside the box. A child can learn to use the power of imagination to solve problems. When our kitten climbed a very high tree and became trapped, I knew I wasn't brave enough to go up there after her. My four children and I became the kitten rescue squad. The little ones were the lookouts at the bedroom window, while the older ones and I tried to come up with a plan. "Couldn't we build an elevator?" asked one of the children. He imagined how his kitten would climb in and ride down to safety. It was a great idea. My oldest, the Boy Scout, threw a rope around the tree limb, and we hoisted up a tuna-baited bucket to our trapped kitten. The imagined elevator became a reality.

Forge relationships with your children now.

Extraordinary responses to ordinary experiences bind family members together. They become traditions and memories. The time to forge relationships with these people who may become your best friends someday is now. We can't get this time back. Make family your priority.

My husband and I used to schedule regular "date nights" with our children when they were young. On a date night, Libby and her Daddy would go out together. It may be something simple like McDonald's and a movie. They had time alone to talk and Jim modeled how a future date should treat her. He opened doors, pulled out her chair, and got her coat for her. Nicholas and I shared similar evenings. I let him open doors for me and pay the bill at the restaurant we would go to. We also rearranged the couples to girls/ boy's night out. Libby and I would get our hair done while Nick explored the hardware store with Jim. The main idea is to get alone with each child every once in a while. Relationships are built on time spent together sharing similar interests and shared experiences.

Now that we have older kids, we reminisce about the fun times we had together when they were little. We laugh over things that are currently happening and discuss how they will make great stories to tell again and again. The relational foundations we nurtured in the preschool years are supporting the wonderful friendships we are enjoying now that our children are teens and young adults.

Create memories, not regrets.

The bible tells us that Mary held many things in her heart. I am sure those memories helped her get through Jesus's suffering. Hide things in your heart now. I always told myself that when my children get married or move off to college, I wanted to have memories, not regrets. Shoulda, woulda, couldas are sad things. These investments in my family and their well-being are already bearing fruit now that two of my children are away grown and living in different states. They call or skype or write to us to share their adventures and hear about ours because they know we share each other's joys and challenges. We are connected by more than our last name. We have history and history can never be taken away just shared and passed on to the next generation.

***Cultivate a spirit of celebration.**

When my daughter Libby was three, she was terrified of thunderstorms. I prayed, "Lord, how can I use this to celebrate your power?" We made popcorn, gathered together in a dark room with seats around a window, and used the storm as a show where we cheered the awesome power of God with each thunderclap. Now thunderstorms are a reason for a party.

Our celebrations range from the very simple to blown out extravaganzas. Inventing a new flavor of homemade ice cream is a great end of the school year tradition for us. Wearing matching shirts that we designed and made to an amusement park tells the world we love being a family. Traveling two states away to our annual Thanksgiving extend family gathering so we can be with cousins, aunts, and grandparents is automatically put on our calendar every year.

Some celebrations are spontaneous, and others come with lots of anticipation. Inviting friends and family to join in the fun always makes it better but there are something things we save just for the six of us. We've had celebrations via the internet using one of the many video chat apps. It helps far-flung family be a part of milestones and joyous occasions.

***Get to know your children.**

The more time I spend with my children the better I know them. No matter how old they were I tried to listen to them and take the time to ask lots of questions. I also didn't shy away from doing a lot of explaining. I worked at knowing their personalities. What was really going on when they are disobedient, cranky, or bored? What did it mean when the middle school child suddenly withdrew? Is my teen suddenly wearing a new style of clothing and too much makeup because they want to be noticed? Is it a sign they need more of me? What are their limits and abilities? Am I asking them to do more than they can or less than holds their interests?   When did they eat last? Are they tired? Are they getting the silent "I don't care" message by my not making a special time for them? What is going in their lives? Do they need help navigating friendships or dealing with a bully? It is crucial that we spend this getting-to-know-you time.

Now that we live in this social media world, I make sure I am on my children's "friends" list. If they are under 18 then I have their passwords and full access to their accounts. Seeing what they post and how they interact with others is a gateway to what is going on in their hearts and lives. I also make sure I know what they are comfortable with me posting. I send them links to articles or events I think they would be interested in. There really is no reason why parents should not be a part of their child's world on or off the internet.

Leave some unscheduled time on the calendar in order for your child to invite you into their world. I find so many parents are scheduling every moment of their child's life. We want our children to have full, wonderful experiences but sometimes we need to be able to get alone with them and look into their hearts and minds and get to know them. Who is this person God placed in your family? Take some unhurried time to listen to them, spend undistracted time, and know them.

Don't be afraid of not being good enough.

We sent Libby to a dancing school near our house. Miss Shirlene had a small studio in her barn. The girls twirled and rocked and leaped for one hour a week. Libby didn't learn much dance, but she learned to love the music. Miss Shirlene modeled creativity and confidence to these preschoolers. The next summer we sent Libby to a well-recommended gymnastics school for tumbling. This was supposed to be a wonderful gym that prepared Olympic hopefuls. It was expensive and terrible. Libby didn't make any friends, didn't learn anything, and felt very clumsy. The pros didn't know what Miss Shirlene knew. Preschoolers need to develop their creativity and experiment with activities. They need to have fun and make friends. They need to be given potential, not limitations in learning and life experiences. The time to get serious will come soon enough. 20 years later our little girl is pursuing her dream of dancing in Manhattan.

Share your interests with your children.

Childhood should be a happy and satisfying season of life for mothers as well as children. Share your interests with your little ones. You don't need to listen to "children's music" all the time. Nick and Libby used to love when I would play my old Rock and Roll cassettes. It was probably because they knew I'm going to kick off my shoes and dance right along with them. Sarah and Alex know I will sing along with them at the top of my voice in the car while stuck in traffic.

Involving your children in the things you love is much more fun for you than trying to just keep them busy. My friend Ginny loved crafting. When she worked on her projects, she gave her girls their own supplies. They happily worked beside her. Sure, it often took longer for her to get something done, but her girls felt so special being included in Mommy's world.

Alex, Sarah, and I share a love of theatre. We have been so blessed to work on several productions together. So often I hear wistful adult cast members tell me how fortunate I am to work with my child and have such a great relationship with them. That relationship didn't happen by accident. My husband, Jim, and I invite our children into our world and make the effort to enjoy life beside us. We don't expect them to replicate our life choices, but we do share what we do with them. We've learned to enjoy life with our children rather than despite them.

Nick our oldest loves history. He learned about historic places and people because Jim is an avid history buff. They spend time sharing what they have each learned or even understand each other's differing opinions. It's another link between father and son.

***Be aware of those cranky times of the day.**

I found that four to five pm was an awful time in our house. The kids were tired and bored, and I was running out of energy and patience. All of us needed a soothing break, but a nap would ruin bedtime. Baths calmed my children, so I prepared a bubble bath for them and put on some classical music for me. Next, I lit candles, out of the children's reach of course. While they splashed, I sat on the floor next to the tub and relaxed. It lasted maybe 20 minutes, but it was wonderful.

Candlelight is a magical thing. It makes children whisper and signals them that this is special. Dinners by candlelight are very popular in our home. Candlelight automatically makes meatloaf a celebration.

Never forget that moms can have cranky times of day as well. Make sure you are taking care of you with healthy food, positive friends, and managing your schedule and stress level. Life hands us enough to do. No one is going to take things off your calendar to give mom a break, so mom needs to remember to do it for herself.

When you learn to enjoy your children and your parenting role life is so much better. Remember you and your family are put together for a reason...to help and love each other and to grow in heart, mind, body, and soul. That means mom too.

Look for creative ideas for your family.

I've made it my business to look for creative ideas I can adapt for our family. Each one of us has the creativity to be the best parents for our children. Each one of us was made in the image of the ultimate Creator and therefore is a creative being. I hope the ideas in this book will get your creative juices flowing. Get together with other moms and share ideas about dealing with family situations creatively. As you get to know your kids better, you'll get better at coming up with ideas to suit them. As the Magic School Bus's Miss Frizzle says, "Take chances, get messy."

Supplies for Beating Boredom

Whether we work in the kitchen, office, shop, or wherever, our job is much easier if we have the correct tools. It's much more efficient to put in a screw with a screwdriver than a butter knife. Children need the correct tools to learn and develop skills and it is a big help if mom doesn't have to run out to the store every time she wants to occupy her child. I've tried to compile a list of supplies that I've found to be very helpful when the "I'm bored blues" hit. These are not expensive or fancy, just the basics. It is also not an exhaustive list. As you get to know your children better you will be able to provide the supplies that interest them the most.

* Open a world of learning - get a library card.

The most effective tool to open a world of books, audios, videos, and computers to your child is also one of the least expensive items you can get. A library card is free and easy to obtain. Children love having their own library cards. Get one for everyone in the family. We have a designated tote bag for items we borrow from the library, so we don't misplace books that do not belong to us. Teach your children to take care of the library books and keep them all in one place at home.

Our local libraries can access on-line, and we can order books ahead of time. When we want to read a special title or watch a popular DVD, I go online to reserve it. Then my family can be sure of getting a literary treat.

*Stock your kitchen.

When you need to have an impromptu celebration, it helps to have the basics in your kitchen. Your family will think you are amazing when you whip up a treat with no advance warning.
Here is a list of some of the items you may want to keep on hand:

flour	milk
oil	eggs
sugar	baking powder
unsweetened cocoa	baking soda
shortening	vanilla extract
margarine	cinnamon
powdered sugar	yeast
chocolate chips	peanut butter

***If you have a child with allergies you will want to substitute items then can have. We have found many great gluten-free items in our local grocery store. Other nut butters or seed butters can replace peanut butter.*

*Items to save.

Save these items to use in projects. Only save a couple. You don't need 15 toilet paper rolls. Every family has a constant supply of these things.

margarine tubs with lids	aluminum pie plates
empty toilet paper rolls	paper grocery bags
coffee cans with lids	shoe boxes
plastic drink containers	newspapers

* Craft Supplies.

Craft supplies make great children's gifts. I find it's better to give supplies than a complete craft kit. I like to challenge my children's creativity. It's fun to see what they will make as opposed to having them copy what's on a box. Purchase good supplies. Crayola crayons and good scissors will help keep frustration levels low. It's so hard to do a good job when your crayon is all wax and no color. Try to store the craft supplies in a neat, but easily accessible place. When Nick and Libby were small, they had to ask permission to get the craft supplies out. I felt that was a good rule for our family. Decide how you want to handle access to your supplies. Clear plastic bins and shoeboxes make great storage containers for your supplies. If you label the containers with pictures your children will be more helpful when it is time to clean up.

crayons	washable markers
pencils	erasers
pencil sharpener	butcher paper or newsprint on a roll
blunt child-safe scissors	tape: scotch, packing, and

	masking
white school glue	waxed paper
tissue paper	cardboard or oak tag
construction paper	pipe cleaners
scrap paper	buttons
rubber bands	yarn
paper plates	bits of material, lace and feathers
stamps and washable stamp pad	iron
rolling pin	play dough or clay
water based poster paint	brushes

You will also want to have craft smocks to keep your little ones from soiling their clothes. Dad's old shirt or an apron works well. You can cover tables or floors with newspaper or vinyl tablecloths to protect them from spills.

* Dress-up trunk.

A supply of dress-up clothes has been some of the most used items in our house. You can get a large cardboard box and let the kids decorate it for this purpose. We also use a plastic crate. You can start the collection with some of your old dresses and your husband's old shirts and jackets. Garage and estate sales and Goodwill stores are great places to pick up more items for your supply. Many stores also sell costumes for up to 75% off the day after Halloween.

Here are some suggestions for your trunk:

hats	large scarves
colorful shirts	bridesmaid dresses
costume jewelry	nightgowns
vests	wigs
boots	shoes
purses	capes
shawls	gloves

Most children love hats. Look for ones that identify a certain occupation. Firefighter, construction worker, nurse, baseball player, football player, crown, animal ears, train engineer, and a top hat all conjure up hours of imaginative play.

Now that you are well equipped you are ready to battle boredom in your home. I hope the ideas included in this book will spark your imagination. Childhood is so special and we, as moms, are blessed to be able to experience it again through our children.

Seasonal Boredom Busters

Each season of the year comes with its own reasons to celebrate. Whenever I would ask my children which season was their favorite, they always mentioned the one we were experiencing. It's such a delight to share the world with little people who inspire me to applaud the passing of time. Celebrating the uniqueness of each season will help you and your children see beyond the schedules and chores.

*The First Snowfall

The first snowfall of the winter is a much-anticipated event around our house. It holds a magic all its own. The common reaction to snow for any parent is dread. What will we do stuck inside with the kids? I am truly not a fan of snowstorms. A feeling of anxiety can overcome me just hearing the weather report. I don't like shoveling, I hate driving in the white stuff. But if I look at the snow through the eyes of my child, I see a winter wonderland. The first snowfall or any time we get snowed in is time for us to stop what we're doing and enjoy this seasonal delight.

Snow Angels

When was the last time you laid in the snow and made snow angels? Have you ever shown your little ones how? It is great fun to lie in the snow and listen to it crunch as you wave your arms and legs back and forth. The real trick is to get up carefully without ruining the impression left in the snow. Sure, you get all wet, but that's when you run inside, put on something snuggly, throw the wet clothes in the dryer and enjoy hot cocoa with a story. One of our favorites is *The Wild Toboggan Ride* by Suzan Reid.

Ice Luminaries

My husband Jim often got home after dark in the winter. One particularly frosty evening the kids and I wanted something special to welcome him home. These luminaries lit up our deck and greeted him. If the weather is right they can last quite a few days.

<u>Materials:</u>

- empty plastic margarine tubs
- spray vegetable coating (like Pam)
- water
- votive candle

<u>What to do:</u>

- Spray the margarine tubs with a thin coating of vegetable spray and fill with water.
- Place outside in freezing temperature for about 4-5 hours.
- When the water is partially frozen scoop out the middle and insert a votive candle.
- Put the tubs outside until the ice freezes solid.
- Remove the frozen luminary from the margarine tub.
- Position the luminaries on your porch or deck or line the walk or driveway with them.
- At sunset, light the candle and enjoy the glow.

Ice Bubbles

It's often fun to do something out of its traditional season. Try blowing bubbles on a cold winter day. They freeze in midair! It's fun to try to catch these frozen bubbles.

<u>For great bubbles mix the following together:</u>

- 1 cup Joy or Dawn dishwashing liquid
- 2 cups warm water
- 3-4 tsp. glycerin (found in drugstores)

Snow Candy

This old-fashioned treat dates back to pioneer days. Adults can watch the bubbling molasses while the children ready the pans.

<u>For 3/4 pound of candy you will need:</u>

- 3/4 cup dark molasses
- 1/2 cup brown sugar

- 4 9-inch pie pans
- large saucepan
- 2 -quart glass
- 6-ounce Pyrex or heatproof pitcher

Have the children fill the pie pans with fresh snow, then set them outside in the snow to chill while you are cooking.

Combine the molasses and brown sugar in the saucepan and bring to a boil. On a medium heat continue cooking, stirring frequently to prevent burning. After 5 minutes begin testing the syrup by dripping some from a spoon into a glass of cold water. The syrup is ready when the drops form a firm ball in the water (245 degrees F.) Pour the hot candy in the pitcher so you can pour it more easily. Have the children get the pans of snow. Working rapidly, pour hot syrup onto the cold snow. When the candy has hardened break it into bite-size pieces and enjoy.

Real Hot Cocoa

If you've never had hot cocoa made with milk and cocoa powder you are in for a real treat. It's so rich and delicious you don't even need cookies. We love it so much we even bought special snowman mugs to enjoy it in.

For four servings you will need:
1/2 cup granulated sugar
1/3 cup cocoa powder
4 cups of milk
1 tsp. vanilla
Marshmallows

Stir together the sugar and cocoa in a saucepan. Gradually stir in 1/3 cup milk to make a paste. Stir in remaining milk. Warm over medium heat, stirring constantly, until hot but not boiling. Remove from heat and add vanilla. Serve warm with marshmallows.

*April Fool's Day

I know most people either do not celebrate April Fool's Day or they spend it playing practical jokes on unexpecting victims. In a house full of clowns April Fool's Day takes a new meaning! It's a day to be ridiculous. It's a day we honor the fine art of being a comedian and as the saying goes "everyone thinks he's a comedian."

Dressing Up

The attire for our festivities is silly. The kids dig in the dress-up box for wigs, hats, shoes, pants, dresses, and put together their clown costumes. Make funny hats using paper plates and ribbons or pots and pans. Let your imagination run wild. Anything goes as long as it's silly.

Face Painting

For some reason, kids love to have their faces painted. There is not much to doing it. The cleanup is easy enough to let them do it themselves.
All you need is non-toxic watercolor poster paint, brushes, water, paint smocks, and a mirror.

The paint smocks are crucial because it's difficult to get the paint out of material, although it easily washes off skin. It is also best to shake the paint jars and give the children just the caps to dip their brushes in. That way there is less for them to spill.

Once everyone is appropriately dressed allow each member of the family to have their chance to shine in the family spotlight. Tell jokes, perform lip syncs to funny songs, or act out silly stories. This is the opportunity to teach your children all those "why the chicken crossed the road" jokes. After the family show is over enjoy a snack and some comedy greats.

Funny Cake is a Pennsylvania Dutch treat that is a great snack to have while watching your favorite comedy classics. Clowns like Lucille Ball, The Three Stooges and Laurel and Hardy always get a laugh out of us. I found our best source for these video classics is our local public library.

Funny Cake

Ingredients:
2 uncooked, prepared pie shells

Cake part:	Syrup Part:
2 eggs	1 cup sugar
1 1/2 cups sugar	1/2 cup cocoa
1/2 cup butter or shortening	3/4 cup boiling water
1 cup milk	1 tsp. vanilla
2 cups flour	
2 tsp. baking powder	
1 tsp. vanilla	

Preheat your oven to 350 degrees. Mix syrup ingredients and pour into uncooked prepared pie shells. Mix cake ingredients and pour directly over syrup. Bake at 350 degrees for 35 minutes or until firm. If your family is allergic to chocolate substitute applesauce for the syrup for a fruit version of this snack

*First Day of Spring

I love Spring. It's exciting to see all the signs of new life. The first day of Spring is not usually spring like for our family here in the northeast, but we celebrate the coming warm weather anyway.

Libby is always most eager for spring because she loves picking strawberries. On the calendar we draw a big red dot on the day we think the strawberry farm will open. She used to cross off the days as she tried to wait. I'm sure the anticipation of one of her favorite outings made it so much fun.

Spring makes everyone think of growing plants and flowers. The following two activities will help develop your child's interest in these areas before they get in the garden.

Egg Shell Sprouts

Materials: playdough, empty eggshells with top 1/4 broken off, damp cotton balls, alfalfa seeds, felt markers.

Have the children mold egg cups out of the playdough. Set the empty eggshells in the playdough, with the holes on the top. Let them decorate the eggshells with markers. If they draw faces, they can later give their eggheads a "haircut." Place 3-4 damp cotton balls in each eggshell. Sprinkle seeds over the cotton. Keep the cotton damp and in the next 3-4 days, the seeds will sprout. Keep it in a sunny spot and as the sprouts grow you can enjoy the clippings on salads or sandwiches.

Flower Presses

My daughter Libby loves to gather and press flowers. She finds beauty in even the weeds. After the leaves and flowers are all dried in a flower press, she uses her pressed treasures to make cards for Grandma. Store-bought flower presses can be expensive, so we made ours out of some scrap wood.

Materials: 2 - square pieces of wood (the same size) approx. 10"x 1/4", 4 bolts 3"- 4" long and wing nuts, drill, cardboard, blotting paper (we've used construction paper) sandpaper.

This is a great "get Dad involved" project. He can cut the wood and drill holes through each of the four corners on both pieces of wood. Make sure the holes line up. Sand the wood to remove any rough edges. We always let our little ones do the sanding and then go over it to make sure the surfaces are smooth. Insert the bolts through one piece of wood with the bolts extending up. Cut cardboard and blotting paper to fit inside the press. Place one piece of cardboard on the wood. Layer blotting paper, items you want to press, another piece of blotting paper and another piece of cardboard. We have gotten as many as 10 layers in our press. The more you put in the press the longer it will take to dry. When all your flowers and leaves are in the press, place the top piece of wood onto the four extended bolts. Tighten the wing nuts. The flowers should be ready in about 3 weeks.

To use your pressed plants for cards or artwork, thin white glue with a little water. Let your child paint the glue on the cardboard or paper they are decorating and arrange their flowers on top. Paint another layer of glue over the entire picture. The glue will dry clear and the plants will be secure. Send the completed artwork to friends and family to announce Spring.

*May Day

The first day of May is a fun day for us. We prepare baskets of flowers, real or crafted, to share with our neighbors. The kids love creeping up to their doors and leaving their surprises. They ring the doorbell and run. We hide in the bushes to see the reaction our neighbors have to our anonymous gift. I think it's important for kids to experience the thrill of giving in secret.

Baskets

We have made baskets out of some of the strangest materials. Making the most creative basket has become part of the fun. You can use plastic strawberry baskets decorated with ribbons. Toilet paper rolls decorated and stapled shut at one end work well too. You can loop some string or ribbon to make a handle, by stapling it to the top. Just about anything can be painted or covered with your child's artwork. Try milk containers, old flowerpots, paper cups, or yogurt containers.

Flowers

Materials: Tissue paper, white or colored, markers, water spray bottle, pipe cleaners.

We aren't always able to find enough flowers to fill our baskets, so we have gotten creative about that too. Tissue paper flowers are easy to fashion and look quite colorful. You can use colored tissue paper or have your children draw on white tissue with markers. Mist the tissue lightly with a water spray bottle and the colors will run into each other creating a unique effect. When the tissue is dry, layer three pieces. Fold the layered paper back and forth on itself like a fan. Secure a pipe cleaner around the middle of the paper tightly. Spread out the tissue paper for a lovely flower. You can make butterflies the same way using coffee filters.

Flower Cookies

Ingredients:
refrigerated butter cookie dough (like Pillsbury)
large marshmallows
colored sugar
colored icing

Slice the cookie dough and bake as directed. While they are baking, slice the marshmallows crosswise into 4 pieces. Let the children press the edges in colored sugars. When the cookies are baked and cooled, spread the icing on cookies. Even little ones can help with this if you let them use the back of a spoon to do the spreading. Place six marshmallow slices evenly around the edge of each cookie.

Planting a Garden

May Day is usually when we get our garden ready for planting. Check to see when it is frost safe in your area of the country. I love playing in the dirt with the kids. We put on our old clothes and jump right in. We've had some neat designs in our gardens. We've had a pizza garden in which we planted everything we like on pizza: tomatoes, peppers, basil, garlic, and onions. My son is not a vegetable eater naturally, but I find if he grows it, he's more likely to eat it...even broccoli and spinach. Try these garden projects.

Flower House

Materials: sunflower seeds, morning glory seeds.

Plant the sunflower seeds in a three-sided square formation placing the seeds about 8" apart. Plant a morning glory between each sunflower. As the flowers grow your children will have a three-sided "house" to play it. The morning glories will use the sunflower stems as a trellis. Train the morning glories to cross over the top of your "house" for a roof.

Green Bean Teepee

<u>Materials:</u> 3 wooden poles about 8 feet long, rope, climbing green bean seeds

Crisscross the poles at one end and tie securely. Sink the opposite ends into the ground forming the frame for your teepee. At the base of each pole plant green beans. Train the bean plants up the poles. If you don't use any pesticides the kids can snack while they play.

*Summer Splash

Ah, summer! That time of year when schedules relax a bit. I have made a conscious effort to enjoy those lazy days of summer. Remember when you were a child?
Summer seemed to last forever. Now it feels like it's over in a wink. Enjoy those beautiful, sunny days. Do crafts outdoors where clean-up is a snap. Read under a shady tree and don't forget the lemonade!
Summers around here can get very hot so before our children could swim, we needed to come up with ways for them to cool off. Soon we had the entire neighborhood joining in. Instead of water guns, we use spray bottles that can be bought in the health and beauty section of most stores. The spray is much gentler, and they do not need to be filled quite so often.

Trike/Bike/Car Wash

We all know how tempting it is to get soaked while washing the car, so we decided to let the kids wash their "vehicles." We gave each of them a bucket of water and a sponge. It's so simple, but it kept them busy and cool for hours.
When the kids are older let them wash the cars. Put on some fun tunes to listen to while you all get out there to clean the car.

Sprinklers

Sprinklers are great fun for kids. They can run in and out to their heart's content. You can use your lawn sprinkler or attach a nozzle to a hose. Secure the hose to a pole and let the fun spray. We play musical sprinklers. The kids march around the sprinkler to music. When the music stops the sprinkler goes on. Whoever gets wet sits out a turn.

Frozen Fruit

You can freeze many different kinds of fruit for a cool nutritious snack. Try bananas, strawberries, unseeded watermelon, cantaloupe or honeydew. My daughter Sarah loves frozen grapes.

*Autumn Festivities

Autumn is the time to slow down after a busy summer. Take walks and enjoy the changing leaves with your children. The days are getting shorter and there are many wonderful harvest treats to enjoy. Rake up the leaves, but don't forget to jump in the piles before you bag them.

Leaf Suncatchers

Materials: waxed paper, old crayons, crayon/pencil sharpener, leaves, iron and ironing board, and newspaper

Have the children gather colorful leaves. Look for ones that are not crumbled or bent. Give each child a piece of waxed paper. Have them arrange four or five leaves, depending on their size, on the paper. Sharpen the crayons and spread the shavings over the leaves. Place another piece of waxed paper on top. Place the newspaper on your ironing board. Quickly "iron" the waxed paper with a hot iron. When cooled the layers will be fused together. Hang the suncatchers in a window for all to enjoy.

Roasting Chestnuts

Most people think of Christmas and roasting chestnuts, but they are less expensive and more available in the fall. To roast them, preheat your oven to 350 degrees. Slice an "x" in the shell of each nut. Place them on a cookie tray and sprinkle the chestnuts with water. Bake them for 15 - 20 minutes or until the shells curl back. Test one by inserting a knife in to see if it is tender (much like a cake). Let the chestnuts cool, but not get cold before enjoying. We like them best with a glass of cider.

Apples are abundant in the fall and so delicious. Try this easier than pie recipe with your family.

Apple Cobbler

Ingredients: 1/4 cup butter
                 4 cups peeled, cored and sliced apples
                 1/2 cup sugar
                 1 tbs. plus 2/3 cup baking mix (like Bisquick)
                 1/2 tsp. cinnamon
                 2 tbs. brown sugar
                 2 tbs. milk

Preheat oven to 400 degrees. In a casserole combine fruit, sugar, 1 tbs. baking mix, and cinnamon. In a medium bowl mix remain baking mix with brown sugar. Cut in butter until mixture is the size of small peas. Stir in milk until moistened. Drop by spoonfuls onto fruit. Bake for 30 minutes. Let stand for 5 minutes before eating. Try adding a scoop of vanilla ice cream to make it extra yummy.

*Make the most out of every season.

There once was a woman who claimed she loved every season. In the winter she would complain about the cold and yearn for spring. In the spring she was overwhelmed by spring cleaning and looked forward to summer. When summer came the heat exhausted her and she longed for the cool breezes of fall. She loved every season, but she didn't enjoy any of them. Celebrate each season as it comes. Enjoy the moments you are given. Remember, with each passing season your child is getting a little older--and so are you! You can't get these days back so enjoy them, treasure them, love them.

MILESTONE CELEBRATIONS

The preschool years are a time when children are accomplishing new skills daily. It is very exciting! There is so much to learn and so much to celebrate. If you start celebrating early your child will learn to applaud everyone's triumphs. Your child will have full and rich memories to look back on. Marking milestones will help build confidence and give your family a sense of achievement. These are important traits to instill in your child for the rest of their lives. When it's time to send them to school or they meet up with the challenges life sends, they will lean on these shining moments in their past.

Milestone celebrations don't have to be long and complicated. In our house, they are often small, but they make a huge difference in my children's attitudes toward trying new things. Libby was very comfortable having her big brother represent her in social situations. She let him answer all the questions and make all the requests for her. If Mom and Dad weren't there, Nick would take care of things. When it was time for them to be split up in Sunday school, she fretted. I told her this was an important step in her life. I gave her a little pink pocketbook with a wallet containing her own homemade I.D. card, tissues, and a family photo. After this special presentation, I explained that we thought she was a big girl now. Libby confidently walked into her Sunday school room the following week with her little pink purse perched on her shoulder just the way Mommy carried her bag. A few years later when she walked into her kindergarten class, that wallet and tissues had been transferred to her backpack.

Celebrate each step of your child's development so when they are adults, they will remember a full and happy childhood.

*First Lost Tooth

The first tooth my son lost sent me to my room in tears. He wasn't a little baby anymore; he was growing adult teeth. I carefully wrapped that tooth in plastic and taped it inside his baby book. For me, it symbolized a new phase of his life.

We've been through all kinds of experiences with losing teeth. One child lost their tooth in the middle of a museum. There's nothing like having your child tell you they lost their tooth while sobbing. At first, I didn't understand what all the tears were about. It seemed the tooth had fallen out and been lost.   Fortunately, after retracing our steps we did find the tiny white treasure.

Ice cream, Jell-O, pudding and ice pops are excellent treats for celebrating lost teeth. They are soft and cold which soothes sore mouths. We have been known to serve ice cream sundaes for dinner when one of our children loses a tooth. Once in a while won't destroy their diet.

The Tooth Fairy

Some families have problems with fantasy characters like the Tooth Fairy and Santa. That is something for you to decide. Many families leave money under their child's pillow when the child loses a tooth. Some leave new toothbrushes, special children's toothpaste or a new cup for the child to rinse with when they brush. These ideas promote good dental hygiene. One family we know sprinkles glitter on the floor near their child's bed to reinforce the whimsy. If you are going to let in the magic, try to really throw open the window. It's fun to crawl in your child's room and not be discovered. It's a thrill to hear their amazed and delighted giggles when they discover your handiwork.

*First Haircut

The first time a child goes for a "real" haircut can be a big event.   Sitting in that big barber chair, covered with a huge apron, being approached by a stranger with sharp scissors are the makings of a nightmare to some. Surround that moment with the right preparation and you can turn it around into a celebration.

Take your child to the hairdresser's with you so they can see what's going to happen. Practice having them sit still while you pretend to cut and style their hair. I remember playing beauty parlor with my sister when I was small. It is a big help to your child and the barber if your child knows how to behave.

My husband took advantage of going to the barbershop with my sons by using it as a special "men only" trip. It's something they used to do together every six weeks since Nick's first birthday. I must admit I did tag along the first time they went, to take pictures and save a piece of that soft baby hair. It was another addition to the baby book. Some hairdressers provide special envelopes for the baby's first haircut. When Nick left for college Jim and Alex would visit the same barbershop and they would fill Mr. B in on what's happening in the big brother's life.

*Potty Training

Potty training -- just the thought can strike terror in a parent's mind. Fear not, all children do learn to use the bathroom. Some take longer than others do, but I've never heard of anyone in first grade wearing diapers. When this skill is mastered it is time for a celebration. Our family celebrated this milestone by taking a trip to Wal-Mart to pick out "big kid" underwear. We topped off the trip with some cookies at the snack shop. I know it doesn't sound like much, but the idea of this special shopping trip is all some children need to motivate them into succeeding in this area.

One mom I know bought plain training pants for her girls. They decorated the "big girl pants with fabric paints. The girls thought their new underwear was so neat they were careful to keep them clean.

*ABC's, 123's

Learning the ABC's and numbers are a preschooler's first academic achievements.   You can use these ideas to either help them learn or to celebrate the mastery of these skills. When we make these concepts fun, reading and mathematics will be more enjoyable in the later years. Remember, every experience your children have will be a building block for their future.

Alphabet Walk

Go on a walk with your child and challenge them to find things that begin with each letter of the alphabet. On a small memo pad write the letters of the alphabet on each page. While you are walking your child can mark off the letter pages when they spot something that begins with that letter. If you don't complete the entire alphabet you start where you stopped next time. This activity keeps little ones interested while mom gets some fresh air and exercise.

Easy Alphabet Soup

Any type of soup can easily be turned into alphabet soup. Look for a package of alphabet pasta on your next shopping trip. About a handful of pasta added to the soup is enough to keep a preschooler happily munching and reciting their letters.

Letter Pancakes

Homemade pancakes are a favorite in our house. They can be for breakfast, lunch or dinner. Pancakes are inexpensive, filling, and can be poured into any shape. For our ABC dinner, I poured the batter into letter shapes. You can also pour it into numbers using the same technique. It takes a quick hand and a little practice, but any mistakes quickly disappear. Plastic refillable ketchup or mustard squirt containers make pouring the letters even easier.

You can use pre-packaged pancake mixes or make your own.

For approximately 16 pancakes you will need:
2 eggs,
1 3/4 cups milk
1/4 cup oil
1 3/4 cups all-purpose flour
2 tablespoons sugar,
4 teaspoons baking powder

Heat your griddle to medium-high heat (400 degrees). When a few drops of water sprinkled on the griddle sizzle and bounce, the heat is just right. In a large bowl beat eggs; stir in milk and oil. Add remaining ingredients; stir just until large lumps disappear. For thicker pancakes add more flour, for thinner pancakes add more milk. Lightly grease heated griddle. Pour batter quickly into letter shapes on the griddle. Bake until bubbles form and edges start to dry. Turn and bake the other side.

For some variety try adding the following to your pancake batter:
1/2 cup shredded apples and 1/2 teaspoon of cinnamon
1 cup drained fresh or frozen blueberries (thawed and drained)
1/2 cup shredded cheese
1/2 cup cooked, crumbled bacon
1/2 cup chopped nuts

Bread Shapes

My daughter Sarah loved shaping bread dough into letters and numbers when she was small. Children can use the letters to initial each place setting or spell out family members' names at mealtime. Use frozen bread dough for an easy, quick activity. If you have more time and don't mind the mess, try creating dough from scratch. You'll have to provide some distraction for the little ones while the bread rises, but the squeals of delight when they get to punch down the risen dough is worth it.

Basic White Bread

For 2 - 3 dozen rolls depending on the shape you will need:
8 ounces of warm water (90 - 100 F, it should feel just warm to the touch)
3 cups of flour plus 1cup more
2 tablespoons dry milk
3 1/2 tablespoons of sugar
3 tablespoons of butter or margarine
2 teaspoons of active dry yeast
1 1/2 teaspoons of softened butter or slightly beaten egg white.

In a large bowl combine 3 cups of flour, dry milk, sugar, and yeast. In a small saucepan melt butter and mix with warm water. Add warm liquid to the flour mix. Blend at low speed until moistened. By hand stir in additional flour until dough pulls clear away from sides of the bowl. On a floured surface allow the children to knead the dough until smooth and elastic, about 5 minutes. Add more flour if necessary to achieve the correct consistency. Place dough in a greased bowl and cover with a cloth towel. Let the dough rise in a warm, draft-free place until doubled in size (approximately 60 minutes).

Let the children punch down the dough several times to remove all air bubbles. Divide the dough into balls for each child. Allow them to shape letters with the dough. Place letters on a greased cookie sheet. Cover with a cloth and allow to rise in a warm place for about 30 - 35 minutes.

Brush the letters with egg white or butter. Preheat the oven to 400 F and bake letters for 15 minutes or until golden.

Tablecloths

While you are preparing the meal, your child can prepare the tablecloth.
Supplies: Paper large enough to cover table i.e. butcher paper or tape several pieces of paper together, crayons.

Cover the table with the paper. Set the table for the meal. Ask your preschooler to take the crayons and decorate the "tablecloth" with the letters that begin each item on the table. For example: by each plate a "p", by each cup a "c", etc. They can also make place cards for each family member using the first letter of their names.

Menus

Using construction paper and old magazines, help your little ones make menus for the meal. They can cut out photos of the food you will be serving and paste them in alphabetical order. When you give your children something to do while you prepare a meal you will find meal preparation is less harried. In our house, unoccupied children get into more trouble than busy ones.

It's fun to pick a letter and try to base a meal around foods that begin with that sound. A "B" meal may include some type of beef dish, broccoli, baked beans, and bread and butter. One of our favorites is "S", steak, shrimp, sweet potatoes, and squash. If this sounds like too much work, see if your child can pick out which dishes begin with a certain letter sound each evening. The "Z" night might just tempt them to eat the zucchini. We also used the letters in each child's name to plan a menu. Libby was Lettuce salad, Ice cream, Broccoli, Beef, and Yams. Nicholas's meal consisted of Noodles, Iced cupcakes, Carrots, Ham, Onions, Lettuce, Applesauce, and Salad. We had great fun trying to find foods we liked and that complemented each other for these meals.

Remember this isn't for every night, but just when you need to get out of a humdrum meal planning mode or celebrate the mastery of a new skill.

Personal Letter Pizza

Most kids love pizza, and when they can make their own it's a fun craft too. We challenged our children to form their initials with the ingredients we used for the pizza. You can buy frozen pizza dough in your grocery store or visit a local pizza shop (not a chain) and see if they will sell you the dough. You can also make your own dough at home.

Pizza Dough

For 2 thick crust personal letter pizzas, you will need:
1 1/2 to 2 cups all-purpose flour
1 teaspoon sugar
2 teaspoons active dry yeast
3/4 cup warm water
1 tablespoon oil (olive oil tastes best, but vegetable oil works just as well)

In a large bowl combine 3/4 cup flour, sugar, and yeast. Mix in warm water and oil and blend until moistened. Stir in 1/2 cup flour to form a stiff dough.   Here comes the fun part. On a floured surface have the children knead in 1/4 to 1/2 cup flour until dough is smooth and elastic. Place the dough in a greased bowl and cover loosely with a towel. Let the dough rise in a warm, draft-free place until light and doubled in size (about 30 to 40 minutes). Have the children punch down the dough several times to remove all air bubbles. Divide the dough into two balls. The children can press each half into a greased 6-inch pan. Have them arrange the pizza toppings in the letter shapes of each child's name. Bake at 400 F. for 18 to 20 minutes. If your family prefers thin-crust pizzas, divide the dough into 4 equal parts.
After the sauce and cheese try these topping suggestions: olives, pineapple, green peppers, ham, pepperoni, cooked and crumbled chop meat, onions, or cooked and crumbled sausage.

*New Baby

The arrival of a baby brother or sister in the family is cause for joy. It can also be a rough time for a preschooler who is used to being the only one. Include your child in the preparations and celebrations for this new life. When Libby was born Nick was only 15 months old. I was concerned that there would be sibling rivalry and jealousy. How do you explain things to a child under the age of two? Jim and I were careful to refer to the baby as "our baby" or "Nicholas's baby." We tried to include Nick as much as possible in the coming event. We celebrated Nick's moving to a big boy bed several weeks before the baby's due date so he would not associate losing the crib to the new kid. My sister took Nick out shopping to pick out a gift for his new sister to welcome her home. She and her husband included him in the decorating of our front door with pink streamers and an "It's a Girl!" sign. Allowing him to feel like he was an important part of the arrival of this new family member made the transition from only child to big brother easy.

When we found out we were having our third child we asked our then 8 and 9-year-olds to help us pick out their new sister's name. Sarah Felicity is always grateful for the good choice her siblings made.

Shortly before the arrival of their second child, friends of ours allowed their three-year-old to help finish the baby's room. This big brother used his toy tools to check all the joints on the crib and the hinges on the door. His dad even had him test the smoke detector in the room. When the baby was born this little guy took great pride in telling all visitors that he made his sister's room safe.

Family Time Capsule

This fun craft makes a great gift from older siblings to a new baby. The real fun will come when the children are 10 or 15 years older and you open the time capsule to see what the family was like when the baby was born.

Let the kids decorate some large butcher paper and use it to cover the top and bottom of a shoebox separately. Tell the children to pick out the following items to include in your family time capsule: a current photo of each family member, a homemade card, or drawing from each family member and some special memento they would like the baby to have from them. You can also include a new issue stamp from that year, a coin from that year, and the front page from the paper printed on the day the baby was born. Each brother or sister who can't write yet can dictate to you what they think is important for the baby to know about your family and a welcome to the family message.

Birth Announcements

Get your children involved in making an original birth announcement for them to send to family and friends. If you have supplies handy, the children can do this project while you and baby are in the hospital. It will help your caregiver if you provide something for your children to do that is connected with this big event. On white construction paper ask your child to draw a picture of the whole new family or just a picture of the new baby and them. On another paper print the important information:

Name:
Born:
Weight: Length:
Parents:
Sister and Brother:

Take the sheets to a copy shop and have them printed back to back on pink or blue paper (or mint green or purple or whatever colors the big sister/brother prefers). Now they are ready for the proud older siblings to hand out to friends and family.

*Other Pivotal Moments to Celebrate

There are so many accomplishments in a preschooler's life that you could have a weekly celebration. We held a "company meal" just for our family when our children began to learn good table manners. The meal was always something simple, but we would serve it with a tablecloth, candles, and our good dishes. Everyone dressed for the meal in his or her Sunday clothes and we played classical music in the background. Nicholas and Libby enjoyed it so much it became a much-repeated tradition.

Celebrate accomplishments and good behavior.

It's so important to recognize when a child learns to take care of things, to share, to be polite and considerate. Don't let these moments go unnoticed if you want the obedient behavior to continue. All that may be needed is a big hug and a word of appreciation. There have been occasions when I have created a medal or diploma to honor the mastery of a new skill. Send your child a note through the mail to tell them how proud you are of them. Getting mail addressed to them is a real thrill to a child. We are so used to correcting unwanted behavior that we forget to acknowledge when our children get it right. My mother always used to tell me you can get more with honey than you do with vinegar. Our children love us and want to please us. Let them know when they do.

Getting Family and Friends into the Act

We love sharing good times with friends and family. Your children need to have connections with people outside of their household. Family and friends are wonderful gifts you can share. Each person you introduce into your child's world brings experiences and lessons that you cannot provide. Adult relatives and friends provide you with support in your parenting. Other children help your little ones develop social skills like sharing, independence, and self-confidence. Encourage these relationships by providing special times for your family to get together with others. We also try to plan activities that cultivate long-distance relationships with family members who live in other states.

Family History Day

Helping your children learn about your family history will give them a sense of belonging. We all love to hear about the time Grandma met Grandpa and the family tree took root. We also love to hear our own history. My children love to go over their "stories." Every birthday we sit down with their baby book and tell the story of how they came to be a part of our family. It tells them just how special they are.
Use photos and stories
We live at least a state away from most of our family and don't get to see them as often as we would like. It is important to me that my children know their family despite the distance. On one wall in our home, we have framed photos of many family members so our children would be accustomed to their faces. We share our experiences and memories of these special people with our children. They feel as if they know their relatives. When we get together they don't spend time being shy but already feel comfortable because they recognize these family members.

*Mini Family Photo Albums

You could also make individual family books for each child. Online photo developers make it easy to create some photo albums. You
can also print photos on your computer and purchase inexpensive photo
books for each child. Cover photos of family members with clear contact
paper before you place them in the mini photo albums so they will not
be damaged if accidentally removed. Now your child can have their very
own family photo album to look at whenever they choose.

Children also give you an opportunity to pull out all your old
photo albums. Use them as storybooks. I think Sarah and Alex are the
only people in the world who love hearing about what I did in
elementary school and the plays I performed in high school. They
especially enjoy stories about when I was their age and how I did the
day-to-day things. When Nick started learning to ride a bicycle, he
asked for a story about when I learned to ride my bicycle. The more
details I could include the better the story. But if I told the story again
and left anything out, he was quick to let me know. It's fun to have
such an appreciative audience for the stories the rest of my family have
heard a thousand times.

*Use Food and Fun

Our family has many ethnic origins and that means a variety of
tasty treats and fun traditions. What are your ethnic origins? It's
educational and fun to set aside an evening to sample the flavors from
the countries of your ancestors.

Our background is Italian, Irish, and German which gives us
much to choose from. It's fun to invite over family or friends who share
the same nationality. We sample different foods. Keep in mind I said
sample. Don't expect your child to make a complete meal out of new
food. It's an accomplishment if your child learns to try a little of
something new. Alex's favorite snack is antipasto because of our sample
dinners.

To make the meal even more special, find music that matches
your theme to play in the background. Go to the library and find stories
and games to share that originated from the culture you are celebrating.
While the meal is cooking you can have your children make their own
version of the flag of that nation. You can fill an hour or a day
depending on what you find.

Grandparents, Aunts, Uncles and other amazing adults

Grandparents and other older adults are a rich resource for you and your children. They provide a view of life that is seasoned with experience. If your children are not blessed to have living grandparents, tell your children about your experiences with these people. Share photos and mementos with them so they have a connection to the people in their family who contributed so much to who you are. My Dad passed away when Libby was five years old. My four children never got to have a relationship with him because his last years were spent in a nursing home with Alzheimer's disease. I make sure they know him through me. There is so much of my dad that I see in my children. I let them know that Libby and Alex's love of drawing, Sarah's way of caring for people, and Nick's interest in electronics and coin collecting are things they shared with their Grandpa.   It gives them a vital connection to my family and their heritage.

I also look for other older adults to fill the grandparent's role for my children. It's so important for children to have multi-generational relationships. Find interests your children can share with their grandparents and other older adults. Provide the necessary supplies, opportunities, and education for your children to develop these interests. Libby is quite an art lover. When she was a preschooler my Uncle Ben was a retired architect who used his time to paint beautiful landscapes. This was a great relationship in the making. I took Libby to the library and borrowed some wonderful art books. We purchased some paints and materials for her for a birthday gift. When we would visit Uncle Ben they had so much to discuss and share. They painted side by side in his basement turned art studio. She looked forward to their visits and I can only imagine the sage wisdom that was being passed from generation to generation while the paint flew.

*Audio Recordings

Children love to hear about Grandma's life as much as Grandma loves to hear about her grandchildren. Encourage grandparents to record their family stories and favorite storybooks for your children to enjoy when they are apart. Tape recorders and blank tapes are wonderful gifts to give both children and grandparents. Children can record their "letters" to Grandpa -- and vice versa! Grandpa not only gets the news but the sound effects as well.

*Using Artwork

Children produce more artwork than any parent knows what to do with. We feel guilty throwing it away, but we simply can't keep it all. What to do? Use the finger paint pictures and crayon drawings as **art stationery**. Letter writing is a dying art form and that's too bad. What a treat it is to get something in the mail that is not a bill. Phone calls may be quick and easy, but what are you left with? Letters can be reread and savored. Start writing more letters to your relatives and don't forget to always share some of those precious masterpieces with those who love your children. It will truly be appreciated and when your child visits Aunt Mary's house and sees their artwork on the refrigerator they will feel so special.

Friendship Tea

I think everyone can remember when they were growing up there was a house in the neighborhood where the children always gathered. It was a place where a mom with a child-like heart lived. She didn't mind the noise or clutter as long as she could help her children develop their creativity and relationships with others. When I was expecting, I decided I wanted my house to be the neighborhood gathering place. What I didn't realize at that time was how much effort it would take. There are times it challenges my creativity and patience. I learned to scale down and provide manageable but memorable playdates for my children. I also discovered what types of activities children love and love to do again and again.

Little girls (and big ones too) love tea parties. I found if Libby had a girlfriend over to visit, a tea party for a snack or lunch was the perfect event. It was so popular it was worth investing in some props. When your daughter is quite small, two to three years old, you will probably want to use a plastic play tea set. Older girls really feel special when you provide real china. Libby and I visited garage sales to purchase pretty cups, saucers, creamer, sugar bowl, and even a teapot. If you are nervous about the girls breaking things and getting cut, Corelle dishes are unbreakable but still are "grown-up." We only purchased enough dishes for two girls. Teas seem to work best with a pair of girls rather than a crowd.

The first time Libby's friend Liza came to visit I was baking muffins and Libby asked if they could have a tea party. When I said I would call them when it was ready they happily skipped up to Libby's room. They reappeared minutes later and it was obvious they had rummaged through our costume box and dressed for the occasion.   No one had to tell them how to have a tea party or how to make it an event, that came naturally and got me into the spirit of the thing. I got out the teacups, brewed some decaffeinated tea in a teapot, and set the table for my guests. Muffins, some grapes, and small cream cheese and jelly sandwiches rounded out the meal.   The girls used their very best manners and were occupied for an hour or more.

Alex and Sarah developed a regular weekly "teatime" with their Uncle Peter. It was a great help to me to drop them off for a few hours while they gardened and had their high tea. It was a regular event for over 6 years. During that time they developed an amazing relationship with their uncle, one that they cherish as young adults.

Here are some delicious treats for you to try at your next tea.

*Chocolate Chip Muffins

This is by far the most requested snack in our house.

For 12 muffins you will need:
2 cups flour,
1/2 cup sugar
3 teaspoons baking powder
3/4 cup milk
1/3 cup oil
1 egg
1/2 cup chocolate chips

Preheat the oven to 400 degrees. Grease 12 muffin cups or line with baking cups. Mix flour, sugar, baking powder, and chocolate chips in a large bowl. Make a well in the middle of the dry ingredients and add milk, oil, and egg. all at once. Stir until dry ingredients are moistened. Fill prepared muffin cups 2/3 full. Bake at 400 degrees for 15 minutes or until light golden brown. Cool 1 minute before removing from pan.

*Vanilla or Almond Milk

If you are uncomfortable serving tea to little ones, try flavored milk.

For each cup you will need:
1 cup milk
1 teaspoon of sugar
1/4 teaspoon of vanilla or almond flavoring

Gently warm milk in a saucepan or microwave to take the chill off. Stir in sugar and flavoring. If you have a milk frother it makes it even creamier and delicious. Enjoy!

*Favorite Tea Sandwiches

Tea sandwiches are thin and delicate. For each sandwich remove the crust from two slices of bread. Flatten the bread slightly with a rolling pin. Place a thin layer of your favorite sandwich fixings and cut into interesting shapes using cookie cutters. Cream cheese and jelly, peanut butter, egg salad, tuna salad, and lettuce and tomato are the most popular items on our tea menu.

*More Tea Activities

You can use the tea theme to plan an entire morning of activities that cumulates into the actual tea. Your guests can make placemats, place cards, and a centerpiece for the table and decorate hats to wear.

To make creative and easy placemats and place cards provide tea time friends with construction paper, stamps, crayons, scraps of material, lace, glue, and stickers. For the centerpiece make available some artificial flowers (or real flowers if your garden can provide them), a container, some lace, and ribbons. The hats require glue, flowers, lace, ribbons, and perhaps some beads or gems. The children will always bring their imaginations. It's fun to see what they will create on their own.

I used the preparation for the tea to teach my children and their friends how to set a table. You may even want to include them in preparing the snacks. Remember any of these activities can be as elaborate or as simple as you choose to make them.

Being A Good Neighbor

It's important for children to understand that they are part of a community. I try to plan activities that teach my children about their community, the people who live and work in it, and their responsibility to those people. A simple walk around the block is the beginning of this education. It's also good for them to know how to get around their town or neighborhood and who is safe to talk to in case they get lost.

*Who works here?

When you run your errands to the bank, post office, grocery, service station, or cleaners, explain to your child the kinds of work these people do and why we need them. Look for simple ways for you and your children to show these people how much you appreciate their services.

Our children love our postal carrier. "Aunt Lucy" would often find a note from them to her in our mailbox when she stopped by. When it's cold and snowy we've been known to leave some cookies and a thermos of hot cocoa for her. We appreciate her and how she helps to keep our community running smoothly.

Secret Angels

It's fun to do good deeds in secret or just unexpectedly for your neighbors. Think of simple acts you and your children can do for the people who live closest to you. Raking leaves, sending cards, leaving treats and flowers are fun and within the abilities of any child (or adult).

*Friendship Fudge

This fudge recipe is so simple to whip up. It's also so yummy your neighbors, postal carrier, oilman, or whoever is the lucky recipient will love you for it. The best part is one batch of fudge goes a long way so there will be plenty for the gift-givers to enjoy too.

For one batch of fudge you will need:
1 cup unsweetened cocoa
2 lbs. powdered sugar
1 cup butter or margarine
1/2 cup milk
2 teaspoons vanilla

Have the children mix the sugar and cocoa in a large microwave-safe bowl. Without stirring, add milk and butter or margarine. Microwave on high until the butter is melted (5 minutes). Add the vanilla and stir until smooth. Help the children spread the mixture into a greased baking pan. Chill until firm (we usually leave it in the refrigerator overnight). Cut into small pieces and wrap in little boxes, baskets, or just paper plates covered with pretty paper.

Talent Shows

Most young children are natural performers. They live in a world where they are completely uninhibited. They hear music in a store and begin to bop and dance. It is a way to express themselves with joy. I wish everyone could hold on to this creative outlet. Why not provide an opportunity for your family to entertain each other? Invite over some of your child's friends or get family members in the act. Provide music, dress-up costumes, and some instruments, and the show will take care of itself.

*Easy Instruments

The simplest instruments are pots and pans for drums and funnels for horns, but if you want to provide more activities let your budding musicians make their noisemakers.

<u>For an original band you need to collect:</u>
Funnel
Ribbons or streamers
empty toilet paper or paper towel rolls
several empty plastic bottles
aluminum or tin pie plates
empty oatmeal boxes
new unsharpened pencils
shoeboxes
rubber bands
large beans
rice
glue
colorful paper
tape
crayons
yarn
buttons

Tambourine

An adult or older child should make four to six holes around the edge of the pie plate. Let the child thread a piece of yarn through a button and a hole in the pie plate knotting tightly to hold the buttons in place. Allow enough slack in the yarn so the button can freely hit the pie plate when it is shaken. Attach buttons all around the pie plate. Give it a good shake and you're in the band!

Drum

Let the child draw on a piece of colorful paper. Use the paper to wrap the oatmeal box. Make sure the paper is securely glued or taped. A new, unsharpened pencil makes a great drumstick or the child can use their hand to beat the drum like a tom-tom to keep time.

Horn

You can't get much simpler than this. Let your child decorate the toilet paper or paper towel rolls. They can even hang ribbons or streamers from one end. Playing this horn comes naturally to most of us. Who can resist toot-tooting on an empty paper towel roll?

Maracas

Remove the labels from empty plastic drink bottles. Depending on the size of the bottle, use the funnel to pour 1/4 to 1/2 cup of beans or rice into each bottle. Put glue around the rim of the bottle opening and twist closed securely. The beans will produce a different, heavier sound than the rice.

Guitar or Harp

Have the children decorate shoeboxes. With the lid removed, stretch rubber bands over the boxes. Cut an oval hole in the lid of the shoebox and tape securely in place. Children can "strum" their guitar through the oval on the top of the shoebox.

*Story Acting

All of my children have always loved to act out things. We would read a story and someone would perform it. Children love to put actions to words. Invite your children and their friends to be the actors for a favorite story while you are the narrator. Try to find a story they know and love that has consistent characters. It also needs to be relatively short. Nursery rhymes and Aesop's fables work well. Nicholas and Libby particularly liked acting out The Tortoise and the Hare in our backyard. As they got older our four children have made us funny videos that we still enjoy watching.

* Relationships make life memorable.

Strong relationships and the ability to nurture and develop them are one of the most valuable gifts we can pass on to our children. There are times when inviting over another family seems like the last thing I want to tackle. The wonderful thing is whenever I do, we all enjoy our time together so very much. I need to remind myself that relationships are what make life memorable. I remember the things people in my life have taught me and the time they spent listening to me, not whether or not their house was spotless or the meal we had. Don't get caught up in the details of planning events. Spontaneity makes for the best times. Our lives have become so scheduled that spur of the moment get-togethers are delightful. Reach out to those whom God has placed around you. They, and your family, will be so glad you did.

Silly Stuff

We've all had those days when nothing is going the way we planned. The kids are cranky and uncooperative. Appliances are not working correctly. The weather is terrible. The general mood of your home is blah! That's the time to drop everything and get silly. The ideas in this chapter saved my sanity on more than a few occasions. Sometimes we need to stop trying to swim upstream. We need to change our direction and enjoy the view floating down the river.

Rainy Day Celebration

Rainy or cold days are wonderful opportunities for fun, cozy times. They can also be days when children and moms are stir-crazy. Here are some atmosphere-changing ideas for both inside and outside.

Indoor Picnic

Pack a picnic lunch and take a walk around the house looking for the perfect picnic spot. Spread an old tablecloth or blanket on the floor and enjoy your snack. Help your children imagine they are in the park or at the lake. Describe what you might be seeing or doing if you were there.

Animal Safari

Hide stuffed animals around the house: under beds, peeking around furniture, inside closets and cabinets you don't mind the kids getting into. Sit with them and describe a jungle with wild animals. Turn off all the lights and let them use a flashlight to go on a safari to capture all the animals.

Crazy Maze

Children love to crawl through and around things. Create a maze through your house using furniture, laundry baskets, furniture cushions, pillows, and stuffed toys -- whatever you have. You can use empty boxes to create tunnels for your maze. See if your children can crawl through the maze in a specific length of time. When my sister and I were little we used to see how many toys we could carry through our maze without dropping them. Little did I know how that would train me for getting all the groceries from the car to the house when I became a mom.

Camping in the Great Indoors

On rainy days my children love playing indoor camping. We started making tents using blankets draped over several chairs or a table. The next rainy day we tried using a rope tied to doorknobs on opposite walls and draped a sheet over the rope. Any of these designs work, the idea is just to give them a cozy, private place. You can put cereal in a small paper bag for a "campfire snack." Don't forget to provide a flashlight. Sarah loved setting up house with her pillows, blankets, dolls, books, and even the family kitten.

Indoor S'mores

The best camping snack around is S'mores, and you can make them for little guys without the campfire.

For each S'more you will need:
2 graham crackers
1 marshmallow
1 small piece of chocolate

Top one cracker with chocolate and marshmallow. Place it on a paper towel and microwave on high for 10 seconds or until you see the marshmallow puff up. Cover with the second cracker and lightly press together. You can also make another version using the same instructions but substituting chocolate graham crackers and skipping the piece of chocolate.

Outside the House

Rainy days are our favorite days to visit our local library. Take advantage of a cozy nook in the children's section after you choose something from the adult shelves or a good magazine to browse. Our library offers a bank of computers with children's programs and a daily story hour. Check out what your library offers.

When it is not too cold we love to walk in the rain. Just because it's wet outside doesn't mean you should stay in all day. Get each family member (including yourself) a bright rain slicker and some boots and experience the joy of splashing in the puddles. Getting out for even 15 to 30 minutes can change the mood.

Backward Day

After one particularly hectic day, I mentioned to Nick and Libby that the next day I was going to do everything backward and hoped that it would turn out better than today. The next morning, I was greeted with a surprise. The kids took me seriously. Nick came down with all his clothes on backward. Libby wanted to know if it was a backward day what was for dinner instead of breakfast. Their enthusiasm prompted me to throw caution to the wind and join in the fun. We ate dinner for breakfast, wore clothes backward, brushed our teeth before eating, ate dessert first, and played before chores.   It was great fun and gave me a reason to explain why we do things in the order that we do.

Color Day

Have you ever noticed what an effect color can have on a person's mood? There are cheerful colors, comforting colors, and calming colors. Why not plan a day around a certain color to help set the mood of your family? Reds or yellows are a great pick-me-up on a dreary day. Challenge the children to go through their clothes and dress in the designated color. On a red day, they can draw pictures of things that are red. Lunch can be macaroni and meatballs with tomato sauce or tomato soup. Serve cranberry or cherry punch. Top it off with strawberry Jell-O for dessert. Use red construction paper for placemats. It doesn't matter what color you use; adding color to the day will brighten the frame of mind of your whole family.

Rainbow Scavenger Hunt

Kids love scavenger hunts. The idea of trying to discover something before anyone else is quite a thrill. This simple color scavenger hunt works well for young children. Assign each child a color and ask him or her to find five to ten items that have that color on the item. Another approach is to give your child slips of paper with each color of the rainbow on them. They need to find something that matches each slip of paper and place it in a laundry basket. Scavenger hunts are great for moms because they can take from 10 to 30 minutes. Lollipops of all colors are great rewards for the hunters when the game is done.

Art Show

Most of us love creating things. Children enjoy coloring, painting, drawing, using stamps, cutting and pasting, playing with play dough, and building with blocks. They also love getting some attention for their efforts. Libby was famous for leaving little pieces of her artwork all over the house for Jim and me to find. She gets so hurt when we fail to acknowledge her gifts. It's worse if she discovers we have dared to throw some of it out.   It is unrealistic to keep every little scrap of paper she leaves for us and there was only so much we could send to grandma and the aunts and uncles. I decided we would hold an art show. We displayed her handiwork and allowed her to decide which were the best. Those pieces became part of her "blue ribbon" collection. The blue-ribbon collection is stored in a box in the attic for her. The art show idea was a hit and prompted Nick to pursue some creative activities of his own. We even took photos of his building block creations to add to the exhibits.

Art Displays

Here are some creative and fun ways to showcase your family's artwork:

- o   To create an easy dinnertime art exhibit, spread your child's pictures on the table and cover with a clear plastic tablecloth. Set the table for dinner as usual. While the family is enjoying their meal, let the children share their feelings about each picture.
- o   If you have an outdoor clothesline you can create an open-air gallery. Clothespin your child's paper to the line. Family and friends can stroll through the rows of artwork and enjoy it.
- o   One family I know has a revolving art display on their refrigerator. Purchase some inexpensive, light picture frames and a strip of magnetic tape (available at craft stores). You can let the children decorate the frames and you can letter each child's name on one frame. Display children's artwork in their frame on the refrigerator door. Each week have them choose their favorite new piece and replace the previous week's selection.
- o   You can photograph all your child's artwork and keep the photos together in a special art photo album. This is a great idea for those with limited space and your child will have this keepsake for years to come.

Pet Birthday

I know celebrating a pet's birthday may sound ridiculous to some, but this chapter is entitled "Silly Stuff."   When we first celebrated a pet's birthday we had no idea when our dog Clara's birthday is, so I just picked a day in January. I picked January because that is usually the month when we are all developing cabin fever and need an event.

We served a special treat, played some games, had cake, and the dog gets cards, wrapped dog biscuits, and lots of attention.

Puppy Chow (for people)

The first time I tried this was at a church potluck supper. Children and adults loved it.

For one batch you will need:
1 cup of chocolate chips
1 cup of peanut butter (smooth)
1/4 lb. butter or margarine
8 cups Chex cereal
2 cups powdered sugar

In a large microwave-safe bowl melt the chocolate chips, peanut butter, and butter together in a microwave about 2 minutes. Mix in cereal, coating well. Place the mixture in a paper grocery sack and add powdered sugar. Shake well to coat and serve.

Kitty Lunch

You can make cute "mice" to celebrate a cat's special day. You can also serve Swedish Fish candies for a snack.

For each mouse, you will need:
Half of a hard roll
tuna salad
carrot slices
M&M candies
licorice laces

Hollow half a hard roll and fill it with tuna salad. Use the carrot slices for mouse ears, M&M for the eyes and nose, and the licorice for whiskers and a tail.

When having your pet's celebration, if you are feeling really silly let the children lap their milk out of shallow bowls.

Circus

I certainly could not leave out some of the fun things we've tried that the circus has conjured up. The circus is a magical, sparkly, exotic place, and children love to imitate it. That's why the circus has been so popular for over 200 years.

Costumes

It's time to pull out the face paint and **costume box**. Let each child decide what role they will play in their show. The ringmaster can sport a handlebar mustache, there can be tigers and lions and bears, acrobats, and of course, clowns. Getting them suited up can take a while. Let them enjoy the activity for as long as they seem interested.

Create extravagant headbands or hats to look like the trapeze artists. Provide them with lots of feathers, beads, and stones to glue onto bands of construction paper. Staple the construction paper in a circle that fits around their heads like a crown.

When the children are dressed in their finery put on some lively music and have a costume parade around the house or yard. When the parade is over don't forget to serve popcorn or animal crackers and lemonade.

You can encourage the kids to put together their own version of a circus. They can portray animals, do some silly tumbling, and walk an imaginary high wire. Take the time to sit and watch their show. The ten minutes or so it takes to give the children this attention (don't forget lots of applause) is helping to build their confidence.

Western Round-Up - Pioneers

Over the years so many people have been fascinated with the Old West. On a difficult day, why not use this interest to your advantage? Dress the family up in hats and vests so they can pretend they are riding the Range. I have found that if I read a story to my little ones and provide some props their imaginations keep them busy. Try reading some tall tales about Pecos Bill, Paul Bunyan or John Henry. These fictional characters can inspire imaginative play about America's expansion. There are children's books about the famous Americans who opened up the west like Daniel Boone and Davy Crockett. Your librarian could probably help you find children's literature on any theme I've included in this book. We try to stick to classics and biographies. By doing this we are building our children's knowledge of history and literature.

Cowboy Grub

Serve cut-up hotdogs with beans in an aluminum pie plate with a piece of buttered bread. Be sure to cut the hotdog slices in halves to prevent choking.   The children can sit in a circle on the ground to eat, just like the cowpokes did out on the Range.

Campfire Sing-along

You don't need a real campfire to have a sing-along. You can share those campfire songs with your children. If you don't know any "cowboy" songs try teaching your children some patriotic favorites like "This Land is My Land," or "America the Beautiful." Nicholas's favorite is "Happy Trails to You." Children love to sing and listening to their little voices is a joy to any parent. It's fun to tape them and play it back another time.

Storytelling Read Alouds

Sitting together telling stories or reading aloud can be a great pastime. It is even more memorable when it is done under the stars or in a blanket fort pretending you are on a wagon train traveling to the Dakota territory. Some of our favorite pioneer stories come from Little House on the Prairie by Laura Ingalls Wilder. Our family has also been fascinated by the travels of Lewis and Clark.

Cars, Trains, and Airplanes

When Nick and Libby were little I quickly noticed a basic difference between them. Libby gave every toy a personality and relationship to every other toy. Whether it was dolls or balls there were a mommy and a daddy and children. Nick, on the other hand, gave everything a motor with a noise. Every toy, whether a vehicle or a stuffed animal, became motorized. It was a very interesting observation. Instead of fighting his fascination with the mechanical, I built on it. It is no surprise to me that he is now a pilot flying people around the country.

Create a Vehicle

Occasionally bring home a cardboard box from the grocer's. Encourage your preschooler to design their own car, train, or even an airplane. Fold the top of the box so your child can safely sit in the box. Provide crayons, colored paper, and glue so they can decorate their car. Paper pie plates make excellent wheels and a steering wheel. Wings are easily created from the flaps on the box.

When their vehicle is finished provide some old maps and ask your child where they are going. They can "map" out their route. Visit Google maps for planning car trips. Try flightaware.com to explore air travel routes. Give your travelers a snack for their trip and a kiss and tell them you'll see them when they get back from their imaginary journey. Children love when adults join in their pretend world.

Birdwatching

I have found birdfeeders to be a wonderful way to occupy my children's attention during the long winter months. We placed two feeders outside the kitchen window so they could watch the antics of our feathered friends from the warmth of the house. They enjoyed bird-watching so much I purchased a bird identification book and they keep track of every new bird they discover at our "birdie snack bar."

Edible Bird's Nests

After one busy morning at our feeders, so we declared it a bird celebration. For lunch, I made spaghetti and meatballs arranged to look like a nest with eggs.

If you wanted to extend this theme, you could purchase supplies at a local craft store and let each child decorate their own birdhouse. Activities that encourage children to study wildlife, even in an urban backyard, encourage them to have a greater awareness of the wonderful world God has created.

* Help your child develop their creativity.

I know many parents who find it easier to purchase a toy for their child than deal with the mess of creating a plaything. Resist this urge. Children need to go through the process of creation. When they use their imaginations to build a car or a tent they are learning. It helps develop their decision-making ability. It builds their confidence and self-esteem. It gives them practice in solving problems. These are some of the most vital traits they will need to succeed as adults. When parents allow their children to develop their creativity, they are investing in that child's future. Isn't that worth the mess?

Planned Attacks on Boredom

Did you ever notice that the anticipation before an event could be as much fun as the event itself? It's amazing the power a red circle on the calendar can have. It motivates us and gives us something to look forward to. I need to plan activities into our calendar to help keep me from getting stale. I also need to make it interesting for me. As moms, it's fun to learn new historical facts and share them with our families. The suggestions in this chapter work best if you can plan them for the dates indicated. Pick and choose the ones that appeal to you and your children. Don't try to do them all in one year or the novelty will wear off. But let me warn you, any idea you try may be so popular you will be forced to repeat it for years to come. Keep it simple. I find ideas like these on calendars, in encyclopedias, or at the library.   You can hunt for some original ones to add to the list. I tried not to include popular holidays and events. It seemed more fun to celebrate the somewhat obscure. At the beginning of a month, I try to pick two or three to work into our schedule.

January

January is a month I need to have some special things planned. There are no real holidays to look forward to and the excitement of Christmas is waning.

January 8 - Singer Elvis Presley's Birthday (1935)

Play some of Elvis's greatest hits while you bop around the house cleaning.

January 9 - First U.S. Balloon Flight (1793)

Buy a helium balloon and see if the kids can get it to float from room to room without touching it with their hands.

January 11 - International Thank You Day

Help the kids make thank you notes for those special people in your life. Take a trip to the post office to mail them.

January 18 - Author A.A. Milne's Birthday (1882)

Read *Winnie the Pooh and the Blustery Day* while you snack on biscuits and honey. (*Do not serve honey to a child under age two.)

January 22 - National Popcorn Day

Try some new toppings on a big bowl of popcorn.

Cheesy Popcorn

Sprinkle a bowl of popcorn with Parmesan cheese or your favorite spice.

Microwave Caramel Popcorn

<u>For 6 cups of caramel popcorn you will need:</u>

6 cups of popped popcorn
1/2 cup almonds(optional)
1/4 cup firmly packed brown sugar
2 tablespoons light corn syrup
1/2 cup margarine or butter
1/4 teaspoon baking soda
1/8 teaspoon salt.

Combine popcorn and almonds in a large microwave-safe bowl. In a 4-cup microwave-safe bowl combine brown sugar, corn syrup, margarine or butter, and salt. Microwave on high for 2 minutes and stir. Microwave on high an additional 2 or 3 minutes or until mixture comes to a rolling boil. Stir in baking soda. Pour over popcorn and almonds. Mix well to coat. Microwave popcorn mix on high for 2 minutes. Spread on waxed paper to cool. Enjoy!

Popcorn Balls

You will need one batch of microwave caramel popcorn to make about a dozen popcorn balls. While the microwave caramel popcorn is still warm, use buttered hands to quickly and firmly press mix into balls. Wrap each ball in plastic wrap and share these portable treats with neighbors and friends.

January 24 - Gold discovered in California (1848)

Put some water, pennies, and sand in a dish basin. Give the children kitchen strainers and let them pan for shiny pennies. You can clean pennies, so they really shine by soaking them in a mixture of baking soda and vinegar.

January 26 - Australia Day (1788)

Invite your children to pretend they are kangaroos and try shrimp on the "barbie" for dinner.

Shrimp on the Barbie

For four servings you will need:

1 lb. large raw shrimp, shelled and deveined
4 slices of lime (optional)
1 each, red and yellow bell pepper, seeded and cut to one-inch chunks
½ cup prepared smoky-flavor barbecue sauce
2 tablespoons Worcestershire sauce
2 tablespoons cayenne pepper sauce
1 clove garlic

Thread shrimp, peppers, and lime alternatively onto metal skewers. Combine barbecue sauce, Worcestershire sauce, pepper sauce, and garlic in a small bowl. Mix well. Brush mixture on skewers.
Place skewers on the barbecue grill, reserving sauce mixture. Grill over hot coals for 15 minutes or until the shrimp turns pink. Turn and baste often with reserved sauce. Do not baste during the last 5 minutes of cooking. Remove the shrimp, lime, and peppers form skewers and serve with rice.

February

February is the shortest month of the year, but it is packed with interesting events to explore. The most popular commemorative days are Ground Hog Day, St. Valentine's Day, Presidents' Day, and Martin Luther King Day. It is also Black History and Dental Health Month.

February 4 - Aviator Charles Lindbergh's Birthday (1902)

Visit a small regional airport where you can watch the planes take off and land.

February 7 - Author Laura Ingalls Wilder's Birthday (1867)

Celebrate pioneer life. Read some of *Little House in the Big Woods* the first of Laura Ingalls Wilder's wonderful books. Enjoy some cornbread with homemade butter.

Cornbread

<u>For 9 servings you will need:</u>

1 cup all-purpose flour,

1 cup cornmeal
2 tablespoons sugar
4 teaspoons baking powder
1 cup milk
1/4 cup oil or melted shortening
1 egg, slightly beaten.

Preheat the oven to 425 degrees F. In a bowl, combine flour, cornmeal, sugar, and baking powder. Stir in milk, oil, and egg. Beat by hand until smooth. Pour batter into greased 8- or 9-inch square pan. Bake for 18 - 22 minutes or until a toothpick inserted comes out clean.

Homemade Butter

<u>You will need:</u>
1 small jar with a lid (a baby food jar is ideal)
heavy whipping cream

Pour the cream into the jar, leaving space at the top. Close the lid securely. Have your child hold the jar tightly in both hands and shake. Keep shaking until chunks of butter form. If your child gets tired, have them pass the jar to someone else to take a turn shaking. When the chunks of butter form, spoon them into a bowl and add a few sprinkles of salt if you wish. Spread the butter on warm cornbread.

You can also make butter using a hand mixer. My dad and I accidentally discovered this while we were trying to make whipped cream for a cake. We whipped too long and discovered sweet butter.

February 9 - U.S. Weather Bureau Began Operations (1870)

Discuss the weather with your child. What is weather and how does it affect us? Buy an inexpensive outdoor thermometer. Help children come up with their own weather reports. Listen to the weather report on the radio and see how accurate they are.

February 11 - National Inventor's Day - Thomas Edison's Birthday (1847)

Point out some of the things we use in our homes that Thomas Edison helped to create. Invite children to invent something of their own. Provide paper and pencils for them to sketch it out. Using play dough, straws, popsicle sticks, whatever items you can provide let them build a model of their invention.

February 26 - Buffalo Bill Cody's Birthday (1846)

On the anniversary of this Wild West Show founder, help your children make cowboy vests complete with fringes out of paper grocery bags.

Cowboy Vests

<u>For each vest you will need:</u>
1 paper grocery bag
scissors, crayons
construction paper
glue

Cut the paper grocery bag up the middle for the opening of the vest. At the bottom of the bag cut a hole for your child'
s neck. On the sides of the bag cut armholes. Turn the vest inside out so the plain inside of the bag is showing. Tell your child to decorate their vest as colorfully as they can using the crayons, colored paper, and glue.

March

March, in our part of the country, is a windy, blustery month: completely unpredictable as far as weather is concerned. We enjoy getting outside again and flying kites. The winter is not over yet, so I try to keep some fresh indoor activities on hand for those last-of-the-year snow days.

March 2 - Author Dr. Suess' Birthday (1904)

Wear silly hats while reading your favorite Dr. Seuss books. Add green food coloring to scrambled eggs and enjoy with fried ham.

March 3 - Inventor Alexander Graham Bell's Birthday (1847)

Paper Cup Telephone

Make a telephone using a string and two paper cups. Punch a hole in the bottom of the cups thread one end of the string through the bottom of each cup and secure with a knot. Stretch the string out and pull securely. Talk to your child over the "wire."

Telephone Game

Have your children line up in a row. Whisper a silly message or rhyme to the first child in line. Have the children pass the message down the line by whispering in the next child's ear.   How has the message changed by the time the last child received it? Talk about giving clear messages.

March 8 - Author Kenneth Grahame's Birthday (1859)

Find a cozy spot and enjoy Kenneth Grahame's wonderful stories in *The Wind and the Willows*

March 11 - Johnny Appleseed Day

Share the American folktale of Johnny Appleseed. Wear pots for hats. Enjoy applesauce, caramel apples, or apple pie.

Applesauce

For 6 servings you will need:
6 to 8 apples, peeled, cored and cubed
1/2 cup sugar
1 teaspoon cinnamon (optional)

In a large saucepan simmer the apples over low heat for 15 to 20 minutes or until soft. Remove from heat. Add sugar and cinnamon. Mix well. Using a fork or potato masher mash apple mix. Let cool and enjoy it.

Caramel Apples

Purchase some caramel sauce used for ice cream sundaes. Core and slice apples. Heat the caramel sauce in a small bowl in the microwave according to package direction. Allow the children to dip their apple slices into the caramel.

March 12 - U.S. Post Office Established (1789)

Call your local post office and see if they will give your little ones a tour.

March 19 - Missionary/Explorer David Livingstone's Birthday (1813)

Talk about missionaries and what they do. Have your children make cards or pictures to send to a missionary your church supports. It's also a great day to play stuffed animal safari.

March 24 - The First Automobile Sold in the U.S. (1898)

Go for a drive to your local car dealership and let your family enjoy looking at all the vehicles. Which style vehicle fits the personality of each of your family members? Is mom a Mustang and Dad a Ford pickup?

March 31 - The Eiffel Tower Completed (1889)

Challenge your children to build the highest tower they can. Provide some original building materials like empty boxes, pillows, and canned vegetables.

April

April showers bring May flowers. While you are waiting for the rain to stop and the flowers to bloom, try some of these activities.

April 2 - Author Hans Christian Anderson's Birthday (1805)

Read *The Ugly Duckling* and invite your children to act it out as you read. Help them to create a story of their own.

April 4 - First U.S. Flag Approved (1818)

Provide your child with an American Flag or a photo of one. Equipped with paper and red, white, and blue crayons, encourage them to make an original flag for your family.

April 9 - America's First Public Library Established (1833)

Visit the library of course! If you can't get out, today is a great day to organize your book collection and create your own special home library space.

April 20 - Make a Quilt Day

Crayon Quilt

Give each child a coloring book page or a sheet of paper. Instruct them to color or draw on the paper. They need to color heavily and press hard on the crayons. When they are finished, place the pictures, crayon side down, on a piece of material. Each picture will be a square on your quilt. Using a hot iron press down on the crayoned picture. The crayons will melt into the fabric and transfer a mirror image onto the material. When all the pictures are ironed on, sew a hem around the material to keep it from fraying and use it as a wall hanging.

April 26 - Naturalist J.J. Audubon's Birthday (1785)

Discuss what types of birds visit your backyard while making some tasty treats for our feathered friends.

Birdseed Snack

For each birdseed snack you will need:

1 pinecone
peanut butter
birdseed
string

This activity is messy so if it's nice weather work outside. Using a spoon have children spread peanut butter all over their pinecone. Put the birdseed in a large bowl and allow each child to cover their pinecone with seed by rolling it. Attach a string to each pinecone and hang in a nearby tree.

May

It's time to get outdoors again. Pepper your days with walks on the milder days. Remember any activity you can do inside can probably be done outside as well.

May 1 - Mother Goose Day

Help your child memorize some Mother Goose rhymes. Have a recitation after dinner for the family.

May 2 - Peter and the Wolf premiered in Moscow (1936)

This wonderful composition is a great way to introduce your children to the orchestra. It is a popular recording in our home. Encourage your children to imagine they are the different characters in the story when they hear the appropriate music.

May 7 - Composers Johann Brahm's (1833) and Peter Tchaikovsky's Birthdays (1840)

These two men graced our world with some of the most beautiful music. They conjure up images of lullabies and ballets. Introduce your child to the soothing effects of classical music.

May 14 - Lewis and Clark Expedition Began (1804)

This is the day to take a long walk at a preschooler's pace. Pack a snack and see what's new in your neighborhood. Don't rush to get somewhere -- just explore.

May 16 - Biographers Day

Help your child tell their story. With a tape recorder running ask your little one open-ended questions about their life. They will enjoy listening to this in ten years.

May 18 - Mt. St. Helens Erupted (1980)

Volcano

Have your child build a large mountain out of clay. Make a hole in the top of the mountain large enough to hold a small disposable cup. In the cup combine a tablespoon of baking soda and a teaspoon of vinegar and watch the volcano erupt.

June

June is Fresh Fruit and Vegetable Month. If you are able, take advantage of pick-your-own strawberry farms. Get enough to make homemade strawberry jam. When January rolls around you'll have a delicious taste of summer to enjoy.

Strawberry Freezer Jam

<u>For 5 cups of jam, you will need:</u>

2 pints or 1-quart strawberries
4 cups of sugar
1 cup of water
1 package powdered fruit pectin

Clean and hull the strawberries. In a large bowl let the children crush them using a potato masher or fork. Stir in sugar and let stand 10 minutes. In a small saucepan combine fruit pectin and water. Heat to boiling and boil for 1 minute, stirring constantly. Pour pectin mixture into fruit mixture. Stir 3 minutes to dissolve most of the sugar. Spoon into clean jars or freezer containers leaving 1/2-inch headspace. Cool slightly and cover with tight-fitting lids. Let set overnight or 24 hours. Store in your freezer for up to one year or in the refrigerator for two to three weeks.

June 3 - Casey at the Bat Published (1888)

Get a copy of this classic poem and share it with your children.

June 8 - Ice Cream First Sold in the U.S. (1786)

Try your hand at making some homemade ice cream.

Tin Can Ice Cream

<u>To make one batch of vanilla ice cream you will need:</u>
1 cup milk
1 cup heavy cream
1/2 cup sugar
1/2 teaspoon vanilla
pinch of salt
1 clean and dry 12-ounce coffee can, and 1 clean and dry 39-ounce coffee can with tight-fitting lids
rock salt
ice

Mix in a large bowl the milk, cream, sugar, vanilla, and a pinch of salt. Stir until sugar is dissolved. Pour the mix into the smaller coffee can and snap the lid on tightly. Set the smaller can inside the larger can and pack crushed ice around it. Sprinkle rock salt over the ice and snap the lid on the larger can.

Have your children roll the can back and forth between them. After about 15 minutes remove the lid on the larger can and drain the water. Open the lid on the smaller can and stir the thickening ice cream mixture. Replace the lid. Add more ice and salt to the larger can and replace its lid. Have the children roll the can for 10 more minutes.

The ice cream will be soft serve and delicious.

June 12 - First Baseball Game Played in the U.S. (1839)

Take the family outside for a friendly game of ball. Serve hotdogs and peanuts for lunch.

July

Our favorite July and August activities are playing in the sandbox and the pool. Here are some other activities to try during those hot and hazy days.

July 5 - Phineas T. Barnum's Birthday (1810)

P.T. Barnum may be most well-known for his circus, but did you know he also built the town of Bridgeport CT., owned a clock factory, and built several natural history museums? Help your children to create their own museum using their stuffed animals, toys, and knick-knacks. Let them take you on a guided tour.

July 7 - Chocolate Day, Chocolate Introduced in Europe (1550)

This is the day to enjoy lots of yummy chocolate treats.

Chocolate Brownies

For 2 dozen brownies you will need:

1-2/3 cups sugar
1-1/2 sticks melted margarine
2 tablespoons water
2 eggs
2 teaspoons vanilla
1 1/3 cups flour

3/4 cup unsweetened cocoa
1/2 teaspoon baking powder

Preheat oven to 350 degrees F. Stir together sugar, melted margarine, and water in a large bowl. Stir in eggs and vanilla. Add flour, cocoa, and baking powder and mix well. Spread into a greased 13 x 9-inch baking pan. Bake for 18 to 25 minutes or until a toothpick inserted comes out slightly sticky. Cool in pan.

July 9 - Donut Cutter Invented (1872)

Take a trip to your favorite bakery or donut shop and enjoy!

July 11 - Author, E.B. White's Birthday (1899)

Begin reading E.B. White's wonderful classic *Charlotte's Web*. Take the kids to a country fair and see the animals. You can also make a spider web to hang in your child's room.

Charlotte's Web Craft

For each web you will need:

1 large paper plate or a round piece of cardboard
Hole puncher
Black paint
Yellow or white yarn
Clear tape (packing tape holds the best)

Cut out the center of the paper plate or cut a round hole in the center of your cardboard. Next, use the hole punch to punch holes all around the center hole. Have your child thread the yarn through the holes in the plate. Be sure to encourage them to criss-cross the hole as they go. Tape the ends of the yarn to the back of the plate.

July 13 - International Puzzle Day

After you have worked a favorite puzzle together, let the kids make their own.

Personal Puzzle

For each puzzle you will need:

1-piece cardboard or oak tag
markers or crayons
scissors

Let each child draw and color a picture on the cardboard or oak tag. Cut the finished artwork into puzzle pieces. Mix the pieces up and see how long it takes to put it back together. You can make a harder collage puzzle by picking a theme, such as flowers or animals. Cut photos out of magazines or print them off the internet to paste on cardboard. Family photos can also be used to make really personal puzzles.

July 19 - Ice Cream Day

Another day devoted to ice cream, hooray! Set up an ice cream sundae fixings bar for dessert tonight. Offer chocolate sauce, strawberry preserves, caramel topping, sprinkles, whipped cream, cherries, bananas, and crushed candy bars. Tailor the choices to your family's tastes.

July 28 - Author Beatrix Potter's Birthday (1866)

If you haven't done so already, today is the perfect day to introduce your little ones to Peter Rabbit Beatrix Potter's delightful classic. Enjoy some carrot salad while you do.

Carrot Salad

<u>For six servings you will need:</u>

6 medium carrots
½ cup diced apple
1/3 cup raisins
½ cup mayonnaise

Grate the carrots by hand or with a food processor. Mix with raisins, apples, and mayonnaise. Chill before serving.

August

August 5 - Astronaut Neil Armstrong's Birthday (1930)

In honor of Neil Armstrong's birthday let the kids stay up late. Put blankets in the backyard and watch the stars. Let them imagine what it would be like to fly into space.

August 9 - Smokey the Bear's Birthday (1944)

Discuss fire safety with your children. Explain the dangers of playing with matches or the stove. Make sure they know what to do in case of a fire. Practice an escape plan.

August 19 - National Aviation Day, Orville Wright's Birthday (1871)

Make paper airplanes and fly them in the backyard. See who comes up with the one that flies the furthest, which one is most original and which lasts the longest.

August 21 - Hawaii Became 50th State (1959)

In honor of our fiftieth state treat your family to pineapple and teach them to do the hula.

Easy Pineapple Upside Down Cake

For one cake you will need:
1/2 cup firmly packed brown sugar
1/4 cup melted margarine or butter
6 canned pineapple slices
6 maraschino cherries(optional)
1/4 cup pineapple juice (you can use the juice from the canned pineapple slices)
1 box yellow cake mix

Preheat the oven to 350 degrees F. In a small bowl combine brown sugar and margarine. Spread in the bottom of a 9-inch round cake pan. Arrange pineapple slices and maraschino cherries over brown sugar mixture. Prepare cake mix according to box directions but decreasing water by 1/4 cup. Add 1/4 cup pineapple juice to cake mix. Pour the prepared mixture into a pan over pineapple slices and cherries. Bake for 30 to 35 minutes or until a toothpick inserted comes out clean. Cool in pan 2 minutes. Invert onto a serving plate.

August 24 - National Park Service Established (1916)

Plan a picnic in your local park. You can also check out a video of a National Park from your library and watch it together.

September

     Summer is over, older siblings are back at school. Now you can devote some private time to the younger kids. Enjoy!

September 11 - Writer O. Henry's Birthday (1862)

Our favorite O. Henry story is *The Gift of the Magi*. There are some beautifully illustrated versions available for you to share with your children. Help them think of something they own that they could give up for someone else.

September 13 - International Chocolate Day

We can never get enough chocolate.

Chocolate Dipped Pretzels

<u>For a chocolaty treat you will need:</u>

1 bag of milk chocolate chips
1 bag of pretzel rods.

Melt the chocolate chips in a microwave-safe bowl. Let the kids dip one end of the pretzel rods into the chocolate. Let the chocolate on the pretzels cool and harden on waxed paper before eating.

September 14 - Francis Scott Key wrote the "Star-Spangled Banner" (1814)

Introduce your preschooler to our National Anthem. Talk about the flag and what it means. Teach your little ones the Pledge of Allegiance.

September 19 - Walt Disney Produced the First "Talking" Cartoon (1928)

I don't usually recommend watching videos but today would be a great day to rent a Disney classic like *Snow White* or *Sleeping Beauty*. If you are not a princess lover try *Steamboat Willie*.

September 25 - Explorer Balboa Discovered the Pacific Ocean (1513)

If you can't visit the ocean today bring its atmosphere to you. Let the kids spread towels on the floor, put on bathing suits, and pretend they are at the beach.

October

There is so much to do in October. Take advantage of the many fall activities that are offered. There are pumpkin picking and hayrides, not to mention jumping in huge piles of leaves. It's fun to rake all the leaves and make a little nest in the middle. Get some blankets, cider, and donuts and have a snack in your comfy leaf pile.

October 23 - Athlete Pele's Birthday (1940)

After you rake the leaves gather the kids for a game of soccer on the lawn in honor of the birth of soccer's greatest player.

October 25 - Johann Strauss' Birthday (1825)

Strauss was the king of the waltz. Why not teach the little ones this classic dance?

October 27 - Navy Day

Gather a fleet of boats and set sail in the bathtub.

November

November and December are exciting, activity-filled months without adding more. Sometimes we do need a break from the holiday rush. Try these simple ideas to break up your days.

November 3 - Sandwich Day, Sandwich Invented (1762)

Get some different kinds of bread such as wheat, rye, or French and combine them with meats, veggies, and condiments to set up a sandwich buffet for dinner. Let the kids create their own version of the perfect sandwich. Don't forget the pickles on the side.

November 14 - Artist Claude Monet's Birthday (1840)

Monet is Libby's favorite artist. She is so taken by the colors and all the flowers. Why not let your budding artist create a masterpiece on the anniversary of Monet's birth?

November 18 - The First Teddy Bear's Birthday (1902)

Place a picnic blanket on the floor, send invitations to all the teddy bears in your house, and have a teddy bear picnic. It's great fun and the clean-up is easy; just shake the blanket outside. Read *Goldilocks and the Three Bears* to your children and their furry friends.

December

December 3 - Galileo Perfected the Telescope (1621)

The sky in December is often so clear. Wake up your children after dark and take them outside to stargaze. It will be one of those magical moments they will remember all their lives.

December 9 - Christmas Cards Created (1843)

Get out the paper, crayons, pencils, etc. and help your children make their own Christmas cards to send to family and friends.

December 30 - Author Rudyard Kipling's Birthday (1865)

Children love Kipling's delightful The Jungle Book. Reading it is a great way to spend a sleepy after-Christmas day.

* Make the activities you plan for your family interesting to you too.

It can be hard to get motivated to plan events for your children. In our adult point of view, there are more interesting things to do than play with Matchbox cars or dolls. Try to look for reasons to plan activities that interest you. Children can tell when we are just not into playing with them. Find things you can get excited about to share. Your enthusiasm will be contagious and you will have more cooperative and appreciate children.

Our children are a wonderful gift God has given us. Parenting is a privilege and a blessing. We need to put family time on our schedules and make it a priority. A trip to the dry cleaners is much more enjoyable when you go after a picnic in the park. It's much more exciting to wake up and think, "Today is Inventor's Day," than to say, "Oh another Monday." Insert unique, special occasions into your schedule. These events will not only bless your family but you too.

Fun on the Run

We've all been in a restaurant at some time enjoying our meal when a child two tables away begin to fuss. In my pre-child days, it would have annoyed me; now I feel great sympathy for the mother of that child. I know how frustrating it can be when everyone in a doctor's office, grocery store, restaurant, or other public place is looking at you to get your child under control. This chapter is about being prepared for those moments and what to do ahead of time to help minimize them. I can't guarantee these ideas will solve every incidence of fussiness but having a game plan certainly helps. Like a Girl Scout, moms need to always be prepared.

Dining Without Whining

Many restaurants are so busy today that you spend time waiting for a table and then again for your meal. Long before the food is served the children are starving and cranky. One of the best tips I can pass along for parents dining out with their children is to serve them a small, nutritious snack before you head out to eat. When you are seated at the restaurant ask your server to bring water in a child-safe cup and some crackers for your little one to munch on.

Most family restaurants provide young patrons with crayons and a placemat to color, but the is always that one occasion when these items are not offered. Keep a pencil and a small notepad in your bag just in case. Encourage your children to draw a picture of their favorite meal. Teach them how to play tic-tac-toe. You can also doodle on a piece of the notepaper and challenge your child to create a masterpiece out of it. One mom I know learned to do simple origami so she could create disposable toys out of napkins to occupy her children.

Play the Waiting Game

Moms spend an incredible amount of time with their children in waiting rooms. We visit the pediatrician, the dentist, and the eye doctor. We wait at the photography studio and school for older siblings. I was at the dentist when I overheard a little boy ask his mom what they were supposed to do before they saw the dentist. She replied, "Sit and wait." "Mommy, my brain is on play. It's too busy to wait," he told her. You can take advantage of seemingly "lost time" waiting by helping your child learn and grow.

Waiting rooms are great places to teach your child her address and telephone number. Sing the information using a simple tune such as "Happy Birthday." Review Bible verses. Ask your child to recite his verse standing as still as possible on one foot. Have them practice some basic skills such as tying their shoes or working buttons and zippers on their coats. Your child's kindergarten teacher will be very grateful if your child has mastered these skills.

While we wait for the doctor or dentist I tell my children to think of questions they have for the doctor. I ask them to show me where their eyes, nose mouth, ears, and other body parts are. In the dentist's waiting room I give them a small mirror and challenge them to count their teeth.

Magazines are ordinarily available in waiting rooms, but they are not usually for children. Using whatever magazine is on hand, let your child search for an assigned picture. Tell your daughter to find all the babies and count them. If she can find more than ten, reward her with a story about when she was a baby. You can also use the magazines for an alphabet search. How many letters for the alphabet can you find in headlines before you need to see the doctor?

Reinforce your child's concept of shapes by asking him to look for items that are square or round. Do you remember the game I Spy? This is a great waiting game. See if your child can guess what you are looking at by giving them clues. If the item your daughter is to guess is her yellow boots say, "I spy with my little eye something yellow." How many clues does she need before she can figure out what the item is?

When we are in a crowded area, such as at a sporting event, theater, or mall, I invite my children to count how many people they see who are wearing hats or who have blond hair or some other characteristic. On a trip to the store, I tell them to carefully notice everything around them. When we are in the car on the way home, whoever can give me the most detailed description of the store gets a special story.

There are times when grocery shopping is quite a challenge with little ones. Take advantage of the store giveaways. My grocery store will give children shopping with their parents a slice of cheese at the deli, a cookie at the bakery, and an apple in the produce section. Nicholas is usually happy to munch his way through the aisles.

Give your children pictures of items you need to purchase or coupons to hold. Explain that you are on a **coupon search** and the coupons are your child's clues. They can help you shop by keeping an eye out for these "treasures." If you are teaching your child to count, ask her to keep track of how many items you are buying. It may take you longer to get through the store, but it will be more fun.

Pack a Survival Kit

Having the right supplies available can make or break your day. Try to keep special toys, books, and snacks for different situations.

Keep some non-perishable snacks and water bottles in the car. Hungry children are not the most cooperative, and you can spend a small fortune stopping at fast-food restaurants for snacks—not to mention the fact that fast food is not the healthiest choice for growing children. Our favorite on-the-go snacks include small bags of cereal, pretzel rods, animal crackers, cereal bars, granola bars, and snack crackers. Try to choose low-sugar snacks to keep children from getting hyper.

Most prepackaged trail mixes contain potential choking hazards for small children. We created our own using Nick and Libby's favorite cereals, pretzels, animal crackers, dried fruit, raisins, and on special trips, chocolate chips. Mix up your own brand of **travel trail mix** with your little ones before your next outing.

It is also very helpful to keep some fun kids' music cassettes in the car. Music is a wonderful way to set a mood. Sing-along tapes and classical music have soothed my children on many long journeys. Visit your local library and borrow some books on tape. Listening to a story in the car is a great way to help your child develop better listening skills while keeping them occupied. We have enjoyed The Indian in the Cupboard, Cinderella, and many Adventures in Odyssey. Focus on the Family also offers wonderful radio theater. These tapes include C. S. Lewis classics like The Lion, The Witch, and the Wardrobe and The Horse and His Boy. One family I know purchased a personal mp3 player and headset for each of their children. Each child can listen to their favorite audiocassette. This mom felt the quiet car ride was worth the investment.

Drawing paper, coloring books, and colored pencils are great travel tools. Your child can keep an **outing journal** by drawing pictures of places you go to. We use colored pencils in the car as opposed to crayons because crayons will melt in hot weather. (Believe me, getting melted crayon off the car's upholstery is a difficult task!) Be sure to keep a pencil sharpener with a shavings collection cap in the glove compartment to keep pencils sharp.

Wherever you go, it's good to have some quiet, self-contained toys. Look for items such an Etch-a-sketches, Magna Doodles, a few wooden blocks in a plastic container, dolls or a favorite stuffed toy, and durable books to take along to the doctor's office, restaurant, church meeting, or Grandma's house. Children can't be expected to occupy themselves for long without something to play with.

Play clay stored inside a plastic container is another traveling boredom buster. Store it in an empty margarine tub or another small plastic container. Your child can play with the clay inside the plastic container to prevent clay crumbs from being scattered everywhere.

Nonhardening Clay

To make a batch of clay you will need:

2 cups flour
1 cup of salt
1 teaspoon cream of tarter
2 tablespoons oil
1 teaspoon of food coloring
2 cups of water

Mix all ingredients in a saucepan. Cook over medium heat, stirring constantly until the dough leaves the sides of the pan. Remove from the pan. When cool to the touch, knead the clay for a few minutes. Stored in a plastic container, the clay should last for months.

Magnetic Tic-Tac-Toe

Another great on-the-go toy is a magnetic game board. You can easily make one for your child using a cookie tin, paint pens, magnetic sheet, hot glue, and scissors.

Paint and decorate the outside of the cookie tin if you like. Trace the outline of the cookie tin lid onto a magnetic sheet. Cut the outline just inside the line so that the magnet is slightly smaller than the tin lid. Using paint pens, draw a tic-tac-toe game board on the magnetic sheet. Fit the magnetic sheet inside the bottom of the cookie tin. Make playing pieces by cutting the magnetic sheet into ten squares. Decorate five with X and five with O. This same idea can be used to make a checker or chessboard when your children are older.

When we are in the car, everyone feels free to sing loud and heartily. When I was growing up my dad taught us all his favorite tunes while traveling to my grandmother's house each Sunday. I am now teaching my children those same old standards, such as "You Are My Sunshine" and "Harvest Moon." Start the tradition of family sing-alongs in your vehicle.

Storytelling is a wonderful on-the-way–home travel boredom buster. Mom can begin a story the kids know well, such as The Three Little Pigs, and let the children take turns telling part of the story in their own words. It's fun to hear their interpretations of age-old classics.

I always made it a point to keep a set of extra clothes, a blanket, a towel, a first-aid kit, and extra diapers and wipes in the trunk of my car. I chose comfortable clothing, like a sweatsuit, that can serve as pajamas on a late night out. When we got home, I didn't have to wake my children to change them for bed. The extra supplies don't take much room, and the items have proved invaluable on many occasions.

On one such occasion, a mom's group picnic in a park, the children were drawn to the creek. Although we were careful to supervise the little ones, my friend's daughter Emily fell in. She was upset, soaked, and uncomfortable. I pulled out my towel and spare clothes. Her mom was able to dry her off and change her in the bathroom. Instead of having to leave, mom and daughter were able to stay and enjoy the rest of the day.

Plan a Pit Stop

Children cannot keep their exuberant energy under control all the time. They need time to burn off some of their energy in an acceptable way. Each day give them some time and space to be children. When you are on a long car trip, break it up by stopping at a park for a fifteen-minute break. We often went to a McDonald's play place after a meeting at church to let Nick and Libby climb and run and have some fun. It's a great reward for their good behavior, and exercise is so important for a child's well-being! Take time to romp with them. It will refresh you after a long morning too.

Be Prepared and Plan Ahead

If you plan ahead for outings and times you need your child to occupy themselves, you will find it is much easier for your child to behave. If we let our children know our expectations, keep in mind their limitations and equip them properly, outings will be much more pleasant. Nicholas and Libby know we can co more fun things with them if they cooperate when we need to accomplish "adult" tasks. Let your children know you appreciate their cooperation and good behavior.

Fantastic Faith Builders

I would be remiss if I closed this little book without passing on ideas for celebrating the ultimate gift you can give yourself and your children. A strong relationship with Jesus our Savior is the most valuable source of joy for my family. If you wish for your children to be blessed by this relationship, you need to actively and purposefully guide them. Through activities like the ones in this chapter, my children have developed a greater awareness of God's presence in their lives. This awareness has blessed not only them but my husband and me and as well.

Many people don't realize that being a Christian is fun. It is exciting. It is comforting and peaceful. It is eternal joy. How do we bless our children with this saving knowledge? The task doesn't have to be as daunting as some think.

PRAYER

Begin with prayer. Pray regularly for and with your children. In order for children to develop a relationship with God, they need to learn to talk to him. When you pray with your children, you are training them for their own conversations with God. Make prayer a natural part of your day. Every prayer is important to God.

Schedule prayer time into your daily activities. Many families pray before meals and at bedtime. We also pray before we drive off in our car as a family or whenever Jim and I must leave our children with a baby-sitter. We have developed a habit, through our prayers, of reassuring our children and ourselves of God's protection and love whenever we need to travel or be apart.

Make your children comfortable with spontaneous prayer. Whenever we hear the wail of a siren, we stop and say a short prayer for the emergency workers and the people who need their assistance. If a family member gets good news or accomplishes a difficult task, we praise God right away. This doesn't have to be long and involved. Simply saying, "Thank you, Lord, for blessing Libby in her dance class," is enough. One winter I had an accident coming home from a meeting at church. Nicholas and Libby were both in the car with me. I skidded on some ice and totaled our vehicle, but God preserved us. When the car stopped, Nicholas, then four years old, said, "See Mommy, God always hears our prayers."

A year later I had to pick Nicholas up at a church about 10 miles from our house It was an awful winter day and the snow was coming down hard. I must admit, I become a wreck behind the wheel. My car was fishtailing and sliding all the way. Libby silently listened to me pray out loud through my tears. When we finally arrived at the church to pick up Nick, he confidently hopped into his seat. Crying, I told my children I didn't think I could get us home all alone. Libby reminded me of how God had taken care of us before, and Nick told me we were not alone. They also said they would pray us home. For the next forty –five minutes my four-and five-year-old children prayed out loud. They prayed around curves and hills. They thanked God for people we knew along our route, just in case we got stuck. Their prayers comforted me and allowed the Holy Spirit to guide me. I was truly blessed by my children. In my time of weakness, God used them to hold me up.

Encourage your children to have their own conversations with God. Begin with teaching your child prayers from Scripture such as the Lord's Prayer and the Twenty-third Psalm. You will be surprised how quickly children can memorize Scripture. It takes patience on your part and much repetition, but it is a blessing to you and them.

We have used the "ACTS" style of prayer (Adoration, Confession, Thanksgiving, Supplication) to guide our children through their prayers. I ask each child to tell God how much they love him and why. Then I ask them if there is anything they did or said today for which they need to say they are sorry. Next, I have them thank God for at least three things he has blessed them with. Finally, each child prays for something for someone else and something for themselves.

Prayer Journals

Purchase small notepads for each of your children. Ask them to tell you the names of all the friends and family members for whom they think they should be praying. Put these names in the notebook. Children can draw pictures in their journal of things that remind them of each loved one. Each evening encourage your child to pray for the next person on their list. This helps your children focus on their prayers more specifically and prevents them from repeating the same prayers each evening.

Christmas Card Prayers

When the Christmas season ends, don't toss or store all those Christmas greetings. Place them in a basket, and one evening each week when you have your prayer time take a card from the top of the stack. Pray for the family or friend that sent that Christmas greeting. You can also have the children contact the friends or family members you are praying for. One way is to make cards to send to the person to let them know you are praying for them. Another, more immediate way is to send an email or video message.

Prayer Pretzels

This is a fun activity to help your child remember to pray at all times. Tell them the following story while you prepare the pretzels. Monks are men who live in a place called a monastery. They spend all their time praying and never leave their homes. In Germany, during the fourteenth and fifteenth centuries, monks always bowed and covered their heads with the hood of their robes. They also folded their arms across their chests to make a cross to remind people of Jesus' suffering for our sings. They needed a way to support themselves financially, so they baked and sold little breads called pretzels. The monks shaped the pretzels to look like their folded arms to remind people to pray continually.

PRAYER PRETZELS

To make a batch of pretzels you will need:

1 package of yeast
1 ½ cups warm water
1 teaspoon salt
1 teaspoon sugar
4 cups flour
1 egg, beaten
Coarse salt

Preheat oven to 425 degrees. Dissolve the yeast in the warm water. Add the salt and sugar to the yeast mixture. Blend in the flour. Have the children knead the dough until it is smooth. Break the dough into small pieces. Show the children how to roll the dough into ropes and twist them into shape. Brush the pretzels with the beaten egg. Sprinkle with coarse salt and bake 12 to 15 minutes.

BLESSINGS

When Nick and Libby were very small, I read an article about blessing your children. I realized this was something Jim and I should be doing for our children. We began that night. When it was time for bed, we tucked each child in, laid a hand on each of their heads, and spoke a blessing on them individually. We continued this special bedtime blessing all through their growing up. If for some reason we were not home when they went to bed, we would go into their rooms later and bless them while they were sleeping. We created our blessing based on Scripture and what we felt we wanted God to bestow on our children. Think carefully about what you want for your child, then create a blessing for them. Blessings are much more than a bedtime ritual; when you bless your children, the blessing will come back tenfold. We said the same blessing every night: "May the Lord bless you and keep you, make his face shine upon you, and give you peace, wisdom, self-control, and joy. May he always protect you and draw you close to him."

Our children came to depend upon this blessing as a token of security and sign of our love for them, day in and day out. Now that our children are grown, they still remember our daily blessing over them. When they are dealing with challenges as adults, I still pray their blessing over them. It's one of the simplest and most powerful ways I know to give my children a daily encounter with God's love and power.

BIBLE STORIES AND ACTIVITIES

There are many fun ways to teach your children Bible stories and principles. The simplest to purchase a good Bible storybook to use for bedtime stories each evening or during some other cuddle time. We have used the Tiny Tots Bible Storybook by John and Kim Walton and The Early Reader's Bible by V. Gilbert Beers. Eventually, we graduated to the NIV Bible. Children love stories. Use all your storytelling talents to make them memorable. Using different voices for characters and changing the inflection of your voice to mirror what's going on will really draw them in. Ask your children questions about what happened in the story and how they would feel if they were the people involved.
IT's great fun to use stuffed animals to tell Bible stories. Alex's stuffed lion became the narrator for Daniela and the lions' den and Sarah's toy horse has been Balaam's donkey. Hearing stories from the animal's point of view is silly but it helped our children remember the lessons we were trying to teach.

Why not have your children act out a bible story as you read it. The story of Esther was very popular in our house. We invited the extended family for our play. Libby loved playing the beautiful and brave queen. The entire family got into the act. Dad plays Haman, and we encouraged our audience to boo him and cheer wildly for Esther and Mordecai.

Use props to help tell bible stories. Nicholas had a Fisher-Price farm set that had been our nativity set for years. We purchased small plastic figures of Mary, Joseph, baby Jesus, and the wise men at our local Christian bookstore. Our children have re-enacted the birth of Christ many times with those toys. I look forward to the day I have grandchildren who march the wise men from all over the house on the way to the manger.

Look for other figures that will encourage your children to "play" Bible stories. We have seen figures for Daniel and the lions' den, Esther and the Resurrection. I have also made clothes out of scrap materials so dolls my girls already had can become some of the characters in our Bible stories.

Another great bible story prop that has become seen as old fashioned is the flannel board and figures. You can still purchase these at school supply stores or Christian online companies. You can also use the back of a couch as a flannel board. We have found felt shapes adhere just fine there. Either buy pieces of felt and make your own figures or purchase premade ones. Let children set up the figures and move them around as the story progresses.

Whenever you can couple a story with an action you reinforce it. Once we helped Nick and Libby decorate a cardboard refrigerator box to look like a whale. We read the story of Jonah while huddled inside the box. Being in a dark, cramped place helped them experience some of what Jonah might have felt. A refrigerator box can be made into an ark for the story of Noah or a ship to tell the story of Jesus calming the storm. The story of David and Goliath can be reinforced by outlining a giant on the sidewalk with chalk. Let the children lie down beside it and trace their outline. They can compare the size of the giant to their own size.

Hide-and-seek is a perfect game to illustrate some biblical truths. Tell children to hide while you count to ten. If your children are like mine, finding them is not a challenge. Most children want to be found. This game will work even if you can't locate them. When the game is over tell your children the story of Jonah. He could not hide from God and neither can we. Read Psalm 139:7-12. God can find us no matter where we go.

God's Love Light

We have used trick birthday candles to illustrate God's love. These candles do not go out unless you put them in a glass of water. Light the candle and challenge your child to blow it out. Tell them the candle's flame is like God's love. Ask them to name things they think will cause God to stop loving them and then try to blow out the flame. There is nothing we can do to "put out" the love God has for us.

Help your children learn the story of Jesus' resurrection using the following cookie recipe. They need to be started before bedtimes, so we made them the night before Easter.

Resurrection Cookies

1 cup of nuts (we like pecans or walnuts)
3 egg whites
1 teaspoon vinegar
1 cup of sugar
Pinch of salt
Wooden spoon
Large resealable plastic bag
Masking tape
Bible

Preheat the oven to 300 degrees. Place the nuts in a resealable plastic bag and have your children pound the nuts into small pieces using a wooden spoon. While they are doing this read John 19:1-2. Point out that Jesus was beaten by Roman soldiers.
Have your children smell the vinegar before putting it into a large mixing bowl. Read John 19:28-30. Ask the children if they would like to drink vinegar when they wanted water to quench their thirst. Add egg whites to the vinegar.
Sprinkle a few grains of salt into your hand so the children can taste them. Add a pinch to the bowl. Read Luke 23:27. Explain that Jesus' friends cried salty tears because he had to suffer on the cross.
Add one cup of sugar. Read Romans 5:8 Tell your children that the sweetest part of this story is that Jesus died to give us eternal life. Beat the mixture with a mixer on high speed for 12-15 minutes, until stiff peaks form.
Read Isaiah 1;18. Tell the children that white represents purity. We become clean and pure when we confess our sings to Jesus.
Fold in the crushed nuts and drop mounds of the mixture onto a waxed-paper-covered cookie sheet. The mounds will look like little rocks. Read Matthew 27:57-69 and talk about the huge rock that covered the doorway of Jesus' tomb.

Put the cookies in the oven and turn the oven off. Let the children seal the closed oven door with masking tape so no one can open it. Read Matthew 27:62-66 and explain that Jesus' tomb was sealed and guarded so no one could enter it. Put the children to bed.
The next morning have them take the tape the tape off the oven and open the door. Look at the cracked surface of the cookies. Let them take a bite. The cookies are hollow. Read Luke 24:1-12 and rejoice. Jesus' tomb was empty! Tell the children, "He is risen."

When you choose toys, DVDs, CDs, audio files, or books for your children, keep in mind their spiritual training. Choose things that will support your Christian beliefs. DVDs like Veggie Tales, audio dramas like Focus on the Family's Radio Theatre, and Adventures and Odyssey were some of my children's favorites. Choose materials that are upbeat, fun, and teach a Christian message. Puzzles with biblical themes teach coordination just as well as secular puzzles do. Bible verses are memorized even more quickly when set to music, and there plenty of audio tracks to choose from.   Our family has enjoyed bopping to The Go Fish Guys and Mary Rice Hopkins. Scripture and hymns have soothed our children to sleep on many fussy evenings. Try music by Michael Card or Bob Carlisle. Some of our favorite books are In Case You Ever Wonder by Max Lucado, I'd Choose You by John Trent, and Christian Mother Goose Rock-a-Bye Bible by Marjorie Anisborough. We used to love browsing through our local Christian bookstore. If you don't have a well-stocked Christian bookstore in your area, you can purchase items through Christian Book Distributors online.

SERVICE

Look for ways your family can be missionaries where you are. There are plenty of opportunities to serve God right from your home or community. Let your children help you bake bread or cookies to your local fire or police department. Call ahead to get an appointment to drop your goodies off and offer thanks to some hometown heroes. Another family mission project could be to collect food for your area's food bank. Food banks are always in need of non-perishables. Consider collecting canned goods from members of your church, scout troop, or neighborhood.

Christmas offers many opportunities to serve others. Each year our family participates in Samaritan's Purse's Operation Christmas Child. When the kids were younger, we would take them to the store and help them each pick out enough toiletries, small toys and books, school supplies, socks, and t-shirts to fill a shoebox. At home, we wrap the shoeboxes and lids separately with Christmas paper and fill them with the items the children choose. All four of our children often drew pictures or wrote notes to accompany their gifts. After praying for the child who will receive each shoebox, we bring them to the designated drop-off center. Each box also required a small donation to help defray shipping costs. Now that my children are all grown, they still fill boxes. Samaritan's Purse distributes these boxes to children in poverty-stricken or war-ravaged countries around the world.

Some hospitals welcome donations of Christmas cookies to distribute to families who have children in the pediatric or neonatal units. We have also donated Christmas goodies to a local nursing home. Friends of ours make placemats for nursing home residents for Christmas or Thanksgiving. Have the children design a placemat on white paper, then take the placemats to a quick-copy center such as Staples and have them copy as many as the nursing home needs.

Another great way to teach your children to reach beyond themselves with God's love is to adopt a missionary family. Ask your pastor for the name and address of a missionary family that may have a child near your children's ages. Send them a letter with a photo of your family to introduce yourselves. Explain that your family wants to bless them and pray for them. Many missionary families welcome this support. Periodically send them "care packages." When living in another country, you miss little items you could easily get in the United States, like chocolate or a magazine subscription. Ask your missionary family what they miss most. On a map or globe, show your child where these missionaries live and where you live. Learn about the country in which they are serving. When the family comes home on furlough, if convenient for them, invite them over for a home-cooked meal and fellowship. WE once hosted dinner for a family serving in Kenya. It was quite a remarkable evening for our entire family. The stories they told of serving God on the "frontlines" were an incredible testimony.

CHRISTIAN CHARACTER

I try to disciple my children so that I don't have to discipline them as much. I look for teachable moments to develop their characters. Often action is more effective than lectures. I also look for ways they can show, rather than tell, they understand a lesson. If Nicholas hurt or offended Libby, he had to ask her for forgiveness for a specific indiscretion. Saying "I'm sorry" Is not sufficient. Maybe he's sorry he got caught; maybe it's just words. In return, Libby had to grant forgiveness. Nicholas was also required to do an act of service for his sister. He might have had to make her bed or clean up toys himself. (All of this worked the other way when Libby was the offending party...or Sarah or Alex) All the children needed to model Christian character. They all learned to responsible for their actions, and to have a forgiving heart. Alex and Sarah learned so much for Nick and Libby's examples as they grew. Don't underestimate what a younger sibling learns from an older sibling.

Use a package of their favorite cookies or treats to teach your children to live their faith, not just talk about it. Tell the children you are going to give them their favorite treat in a few minutes, but first, they need to tell you about the treat. What does it smell like, feel like, look like, taste like? Let them answer all your questions. When they are finished, serve the snack. Ask the children why eating the snack is better than talking about the snack. Tell them it is the same way with our belief in Jesus. We can talk about Jesus but talking doesn't give us the same benefits as actually having Jesus in our lives. We have to live our faith to get all the blessings Jesus has for us. Discuss the blessings your family has experienced. If your children have not accepted Jesus as their Savior yet, now is a great time to invite them to do so.

It is a very special honor to lead your child to Christ. Don't wait for them to learn about Jesus in church or Sunday School. As a parent, God has called you to bring this very special person to Him. It is a very special blessing.

Look for special moments to point out God's love, provision, and handiwork to your children. Throughout this book, you will note occasions to acknowledge God. When you explore your garden, gaze at a starry sky, or tell your child your life stories, do it from a godly perspective. Let your child hear you thinking god for all the wonders and blessings around you.

Take time to develop a strong relationship with Jesus yourself. Through this relationship not only will you have eternal life, but you will have the power of the Holy Spirit to help you be the best parent you can be. What better blessing can we give our little ones than the joy of the Lord? As your children see you grow in the Lord, they will want to know him better too. As you and your children grow spiritually, you will find parenting gets easier. It becomes fun and purposeful. You will find your creativity abounding and your children showing a more teachable spirit. Always remember that God is your parenting partner and loves your child even more than you do. I need to lean on this truth so many times during my mothering journey. Children take us so much of our time and energy. Learn to see God through the gifts of your children, instead of in spite of them.

It is my prayer that through this little book you and your family are able to grow closer to each other and   God – have fun, memorable moments doing it. Life is an exciting adventure and a blessing – enjoy it!

About the Author

Barbara Vogelgesang has been speaking, performing, teaching, and clowning for 30 years. She has toured with Ringling Bros. and Barnum and Bailey Circus and toured throughout the U.S. Canada, and Japan. Barbara and her husband, Jim, are the proud parents of Nicholas, Libby, Sarah, and Alex. She holds a journalism degree from St. John's University in NYC and has attended Ringling Bros Barnum and Bailey's Clown College. Barbara has worked in the public relations departments of Estee Lauder and Madison Square Garden. Currently, she is a teaching artist for Touchstone Theatre's Young Playwright's Lab. She also directs and costumes local theatre productions. Barbara and her husband reside in beautiful, rural Pennsylvania with their playful pup, Zelma, and lots of visits from their now-grown children. She loves being creative and having adventures with family and friends.

About the Illustrator

Emma Engler has always loved the arts, no matter what form. She's been acting for almost 10 years, singing and playing guitar as well. Drawing has always been a favorite hobby of Emma's, using it in her writing and just for fun. She is currently a sophomore at the Lehigh Valley Charter High School for the Arts, majoring in literary arts. Emma loves world-building and creating characters in her original stories and screenplays. She hopes to attend college for film after graduation, and one day write and direct movies of her own. Presently, she and her parents, younger brother, evil cat, posh rabbit, and insanely energetic puppy all live happily together in the Pocono Mts. of Pennsylvania.